Ancient Records and the Structure of Genesis

Ancient Records and the Structure of Genesis

A Case for Literary Unity

P. J. Wiseman
Edited by D. J. Wiseman

Thomas Nelson Publishers
Nashville • Camden • New York

Published in Nashville, Tennessee by Thomas Nelson, Inc.,
and distributed in Canada by Lawson Falle, Ltd., Cam-
bridge, Ontario.

Printed in the United States of America.

A revised version, originally published in 1936, as *New
Discoveries in Babylonia About Genesis*. It was reissued in
1977 by Marshall, Morgan, and Scott as part of *Clues to
Creation in Genesis*.

The tablet of the *Atrahasis Epic* is pictured by kind permission of the Trustees of the British Museum.

Unless otherwise noted, Scripture quotations are from the
King James Version.

Library of Congress Cataloging in Publication Data

Wiseman, P. J., 1888-1948.
    Ancient records and the structure of Genesis.

    1. Bible. O.T. Genesis—Criticism, interpretation, etc.
2. Bible. O.T. Genesis—Evidences, authority, etc. 3. Bible.
O.T. Genesis—Antiquities. 4. Assyro-Babylonian literature—Relation to the Old Testament. 5. Iraq—Antiquities.
I. Wiseman, D. J. (Donald John) II. Title.

BS1235.2.W57 1985   222'.11066   84-29564
ISBN 0-8407-7502-4

Contents

Foreword
by
D. J. Wiseman

Former Professor of Assyriology in the University of London and Assistant Keeper, Department of Western Asiatic Antiquities, The British Museum.

In response to a growing number of requests, the study written by my late father, P. J. Wiseman,[1] is presented here in a single volume. It originally appeared as *New Discoveries in Babylonia about Genesis* in 1936. Despite publication in "war economy" format and in a limited edition, new printings were immediately required. These were followed by translations into German (*Die Entstehung der Genesis*, Wuppertal, 1958) and into Dutch (*Ontdekkingen over Genesis*, Groningen, 1960). Reference to his writings are made in a number of books (for example, R. K. Harrison, *Introduction to the Old*

---

[1] Air Commodore P. J. Wiseman, CBE, RAF (1888-1948). He was also president of the Victoria Institute and the Crusader's Union in England.

Testament, 1969, which summarizes the book on pp. 545-53). These have increased the demand for a reprint.

My father's interest as a Bible student was quickened by his residence in the Middle East, especially during 1923-25 and 1931-33 when in Iraq. He read extensively and took the opportunity of visiting the principal excavations; these included the British Museum and University Museum of Pensylvania expedition to Ur under Sir Leonard Wooley and that of the University of Oxford Ashmolean Museum at Kish under Professor S. H. Langdon. He had many discussions with these and other scholars there (especially Professor Cyril Gadd). While he himself did not read the cuneiform scripts and had a limited knowledge of classical Hebrew, he carefully checked his theories with competent scholars. His enthusiasm was in no small measure the encouragement to me to enter these specialized fields of archaeology and ancient Semitic languages, and we often discussed his ideas in their formative stages.

P. J. Wiseman's primary idea is a simple one. Taking his cue from the recurrent "catch-lines" or colophons in Genesis of the form, "These are the family histories (generations) of...," he examines them as clues to the literary structure of Genesis and as indicative of its origin and transmission. He takes the Genesis narratives as they stand and relates them to well-attested ancient literary methods. My father always thought that such a subjective theory as that of the Wellhausen school would hardly have been conceived or copied had the many literary tests (among them thousands of cuneiform tablets which have since been discovered) been known at that time.

Since this book was first written there have been many more colophons discovered among the cuneiform texts which have been found in Babylonia. They have been published by H. Hunger, *Babylonische und Assyrische*

Kolophone (1968) and by E. Leichty, "The Colophon" in *Studies Presented to A. L. Oppenheim* (1964), pp. 147-54. These substantiate the references to this scribal device which is the "key" to the elucidation of the documents which were composed in Genesis.

Recent discoveries of Semitic literature from Syria and Mesopotamia, among them many dated texts *ca.* 2300 BC—notably the finds in 1975-76 from Tell Mardiḥ (Ebla) and, from a millennium later, the Akkadian texts from Ras Shamra (Ugarit)—show the continuity in tradition both of scribal education and literary practices. In many instances tablets show them to have continued virtually unchanged for a further two millenniums. Unlike the Wellhausen theories, based on subjective assessment of the Hebrew text alone, these extra-biblical documents give us fixed and dated points along this stream of tradition.

Since it was no part of the original purpose to provide a survey of archaeology in relation to the book of Genesis, no attempt has been made, or is necessary to the main argument, to bring archaeological detail up to date. A number of minor changes have been made for the sake of clarity. In the main, however, it has been thought desirable to adhere as closely as possible to the author's views as originally expressed. For this reason the King James Version has been left as the basis of all quotations from Scripture.

To the present writer the particular value of this theory in relation to Genesis is the implication of the early use of writing, with the possibility that Genesis 1-37 could be a transcript from the oldest series of written records.

Preface
by
R. K. Harrison

Bishops Frederick and Heber Wilkinson Chair of Old Testament at Wycliffe College, Toronto, Ontario.

The position that the book of Genesis occupies as the first of "five-fifths" of the Torah or Law of Moses has understandably caused it to be regarded as the work of the esteemed Hebrew lawgiver. This was the traditional attribution among both Jews and early Christians, even though Genesis itself is strictly an anonymous work that, unlike the other Pentateuchal compositions, makes no claim to Mosaic authorship.

While some medieval Jewish exegetes purported to recognize the presence of "late" insertions in the Pentateuch, they did not question the Mosaic authorship of Genesis. Only in the seventeenth century did serious questions begin to be raised about the composition of Genesis, and even these dealt with source criticism rather than with the author himself. Thus Jean Astruc (1684-1766) published an anonymous work which maintained that the material in Genesis had been transmitted either in written or oral form up to the time of Moses, and that he organized these ancient sources by making a chronological narrative out of them.

Astruc was probably much closer to the truth of the matter than he realized. Had he been in possession of information that has since come to light, he could well have performed a valuable service to the scholarly community and others in isolating or characterizing the underlying literary sources of Genesis. But having no option save to speculate, he marred his observations from the beginning by speaking of "duplicate narratives" of the Creation and the Flood in Genesis. Even a casual observation of the material involved shows that the sections are not in fact duplicates, but constitute passages in which the longer accounts represent expansions of summary statements, as for example in connection with the creation of humanity (Gen. 1:27 and 2:7-23).

Quite without any warrant in terms of objective, factual data, Astruc held that the Genesis material was presented in incorrect chronological order, and accordingly he set about remedying the situation. He noted that God was referred to in the Hebrew as both Elohim and Jehovah, and following an earlier suggestion that these names might provide a clue to source analysis, he collected all the verses in which Elohim appeared and tabulated the data in columnar form. This material constituted for him the basic documentary source of Genesis, but it did not by any means exhaust the content of the book. Accordingly he made another column out of the verses that spoke of God as Jehovah, and to complete his work he compiled two more columns of verses, one consisting mostly of what he regarded as "repetitions" and the other of "non-Israelite" material.

Astruc felt that he had found the solution to the problem of the literary sources employed by Moses in the compilation of Genesis, and thereafter he expended considerable effort in the defense of the Mosaic authorship of the book. But after some time he began to realize that the divine names were inadequate as criteria for a proper source analysis of Genesis, only to discover that by then he had established a pattern of investigation that subsequent European scholarship was to follow and modify.

In 1800 a Scottish Roman Catholic scholar named Geddes set aside Astruc's Elohistic and Jehovistic source "documents" and instead advanced a "fragmentary hypothesis" which maintained that an editor had compiled the Pentateuch from a mass of literary fragments during the Solomonic period. J. S. Vater in 1805 went even further by assigning the composition of the Pentateuch to the exilic period. The rationalist writer De Wette maintained the superiority of Astruc's documentary theory over the fragmentary hypothesis and commended his choice of Elohistic material as the basic source for Genesis.

The entirely subjective nature of such literary analysis naturally led to considerable conflict of opinion among those who interested themselves in advancing their own views on the manner in which Genesis and the other Pentateuchal books were compiled. Conservative scholars adhered to the traditional view of Moses as the author of the works attributed to him, while the more rationalistic writers speculated freely about literary origins and sources. By the middle of the nineteenth century liberal scholarship had, to its own satisfaction, isolated four main Pentateuchal sources comprising a Jehovistic (J) document, an Elohistic (E) source, a Priestly (P) compilation, and the book of Deuteronomy (D). These supposedly underlying sources of the Pentateuch, of which the only valid one is Deuteronomy, were formulated into a developmental hypothesis as a result of the writings of

K. H. Graf in 1865 and Julius Wellhausen in 1877.

Thereafter this view of Pentateuchal origins became the standard explanation provided by liberal scholarship for the origin and growth of the entire Pentateuch. Based on the entirely erroneous assumption that writing was only invented about the time of David (*ca.* 1000 BC), the four postulated documents were assigned to periods from the ninth century BC to the post-exilic period; the completed Pentateuch, duly assembled and edited by numerous anonymous redactors, supposedly being in extant form by about 200 BC. As far as Genesis was concerned, the consensus of opinion distributed the material broadly between the hypothetical J and E sources, with the inclusion of prominent sections from the Priestly collection and, according to some literary critics, the addition of an L source made up of fragments that "interrupted" the main J narrative.

These views encountered a storm of criticism from the more orthodox Christians, as well as engendering a great deal of internal criticism directed by liberal scholars at their radical associates. But the evolutionary concept which the works of Graf and Wellhausen enshrined was at that time an essential ingredient of the spirit of the age, and as a result objectors to the "most assured results of literary criticism" were dismissed as obscurantists who were impeding the progress of scientific knowledge. The Graf-Wellhausen hypothesis, as the most developed form of rationalistic literary criticism was called, became accepted as scholarly orthodoxy, and is still taught by people of liberal persuasion, albeit in a considerably modified form from its classical expression.

While the kind of literary critical study that has been surveyed briefly could be hailed as representing the best intellectual efforts of the age from which it emerged, more sober assessments, based in part upon information that was either not apparent or available until the twentieth century, have demonstrated certain fundamental weaknesses in the theoretical principles that motivated the work. First and foremost, critical studies of the Enlightenment period were based upon a Greek way of thinking, which in the realm of natural philosophy consisted of formulating a priori general hypotheses of an unsupportable kind. Since this approach was roundly condemned as unscientific in a Greek essay on ancient medicine, dating from the time of Hippocrates (460-357 BC), it is ironic that the advocates of the Graf-Wellhausen hypothesis claimed their efforts represented "scientific literary criticism."

As bad as it was to be promoting purely speculative and subjective notions, it was even worse to recognize that at best these hypotheses were strictly unsupportable generalizations. The plain fact is that after more than a century of close investigation, scholars have not merely failed to demonstrate the existence of J, E, P, L, and the like but have not even agreed upon the precise content of these alleged "documents." As remarked above, the only credible source in the entire Graf-Wellhausen hypothesis is D, the book of Deuteronomy, which was already in existence as a complete document long before any form of criticism arose.

An equally grave methodological error was an attitude of cross-cultural extrapolation, which imagined that ancient Near Eastern culture had been fashioned in terms of modern European traditions and that it must be evaluated accordingly. Thus in the process of formulating their propositions about authorship and literary sources it apparently never occurred to the European savants that it might be desirable for them to discover just how information might have been recorded and transmitted in the period represented by the book of Genesis and how documents were actually formulated.

Indeed, it was only when the archaeological discoveries of the nineteenth and twentieth centuries began to reveal something of the character of Near Eastern antiquity that embarrassing gaffes began to be apparent in literary-critical methodology. Thus the assumption that writing only came into vogue in the Davidic period was shown to be wide of the mark by over 2000 years, originating about 3300 BC. The cultures of Mesopotamia as represented in Genesis proved to have been advanced rather than primitive or "evolving" in character, and in some cases already going to decline. Had any one of the literary critics studied the Koran carefully as a composition that stood firmly in the tradition of Semitic writings, he could not possibly have used the names of God as criteria for identifying and recovering supposed "documents," since he would have had almost one hundred such elements as supposed sources for the Koran. Needless to say, Islamic scholars quite properly ridicule any other notion than that the Koran is the unified work of a single author.

There will doubtless be many people reading these observations who will want to dismiss the whole question of the literary criticism of the Old Testament as a pointless and unproductive expenditure of time and energy. "Why," they may say, "is it necessary to be bothered with such questions? Is it surely not sufficient to accept the material as it stands and try to discover the spiritual message without any concern for splitting up the narratives into supposed sources?" The answer is that for some persons there is absolutely no need for a knowledge of the component parts, real or supposed, of Genesis or any other biblical book, just as there is no necessity for them to know what the ingredients are in, say, a bottle of cough medicine, or the pharmacological principles by which they are compounded.

But if one looks carefully at Scripture, it is evident that in certain places quite obvious and specific methods were employed in the compilation of the materials, and that since these reflect accredited procedures used by the ancient scribes, they must in fact be studied carefully if we are to avoid the mistakes and erroneous conjectures of the nineteenth-century European scholars, and examine the transmission and compilation of sources in terms of ancient Near Eastern rather than modern European traditions.

A glance at the books of Chronicles will suffice to show how some of the sources on which the author drew for information have been preserved by title in the text. In the books of Kings and Chronicles, the synchronistic lists of rulers in Israel and Judah were formulated professionally by scribes whose recording techniques have only recently become known to western scholars. By studying these works our understanding of the way in which records were made and preserved in the Near East has been enriched considerably.

If, then, it is at all legitimate to look for sources in a work such as Genesis, it is important for the investigator to be absolutely sure that such elements are realistic and are not the product of unbridled or unreasoned speculation. There is an enormous amount of objective archaeological data available for study which has furnished valuable information about life in Near Eastern antiquity, and it is against this background, and not one of an untestable intellectual proposition, that all future source studies must be conducted.

This concept had commended itself to one German scholar, Hermann Gunkel, who was impressed by the necessity for understanding the life-situation in any evaluation of the various literary forms in Scripture. Unfortunately Gunkel himself failed completely in his attempt to interpret the significance of the Genesis narratives by thinking of them as having been passed down originally as independent oral sagas associated with some particular individual. Had Gunkel been more familiar with the typical environmental form of much of ancient Near Eastern literature, he might well have come to vastly different conclusions about the sources of Genesis; particularly if he had been able to use the form-critical techniques that he was commending to isolate genuine literary sources in the book of Genesis.

Archaeological discoveries have produced thousands of clay tablets from Mesopotamia, written in a strange wedge-shaped script. In many instances the tablets that have been recovered exhibit a specific literary form comprising a title, followed by the body of the text and concluding with a colophon. This latter feature generally contained the name of the owner or scribe and some attempt at dating. Since the colophon comes at the end of a tablet or a series of tablets, it naturally refers to material that precedes it on the tablet.

Using these archaeological records as a pattern of specific literary activity, it is possible for anyone to isolate eleven sections of material from Genesis once the colophon has been identified. The presence of a colophon is indicated by the recurring phrase, "These are the generations (tōlēdōt) of...," the Hebrew phrase meaning "histories, family histories, genealogies." The juxtaposition of the various sections with the minimum of editorial intervention presents a history of mankind from creation to the period of Joseph. A separate concurrent section with an Egyptian rather than a Mesopotamian or Canaanite cultural background completed the extant book of Genesis, and may well have been compiled by the scribe who assembled the tablet material.

While other scholars may perhaps have felt that sections of the narratives comprising Genesis 1:1—37:2a bore the general form of Mesopotamian tablets, they did not pursue the matter to any extent. Such an enterprise was left to the late Air Commodore P. J. Wiseman, who during a tour of duty in Mesopotamia became intrigued by the relationship between the literary form of ancient Babylonian tablets with their catch-lines, scribal datings, genealogies, and colophons, and the eleven sections of Genesis which he was able to isolate once he had recognized the colophon.

Wiseman's work represents an important forward movement in an understanding of the source criticism and compilation of Genesis against a background of the Babylonian "life-situation." As opposed to purely hypothetical "documents," the reader is introduced by Wiseman's book to realistic literary sources for Genesis that reflect accurately the culture and scribal traditions of highly literate peoples who did not hesitate to record in writing the important events of their day.

Air Commodore P. J. Wiseman's book, first published in 1936, is now presented in a form edited by his son, Professor D. J. Wiseman, who is himself a renowned Near Eastern scholar. After a brief description of archaeological discoveries in Babylonia, the author examines ancient scribal methods before discussing the phrase, "These are the generations (tōlēdōt) of...," which for him holds the answer to the literary structure of the book of Genesis. After studying his contention that this great work was written for the most part on clay tablets by people who were well informed about the events which they narrated, it is difficult to resist the conclusion that there could possibly be any other credible way in which the book was compiled. Unlike the speculators of an earlier age of study, Wiseman brings a lengthy examination of the ancient literary forms of Mesopotamian tablets to bear upon the problems of the compilation of Genesis. By adducing comparable literary materials from secular society to support his thesis, he brings a greater degree of realism to his task than is achieved by any other treatment of the sources underlying Genesis.

I

Introduction

This book is the outcome of studies in archaeology, completed while the author was working in Iraq. The investigation of the problems of the book of Genesis in its ancient environment, and in the light of the mass of facts regarding ancient literary methods, throws an entirely new light on the problem of its nature and authorship.

The aim is to state as simply as possible the evidence which Genesis has to give concerning its own origin and composition. To many it will appear surprising that Genesis has anything whatever to say for itself regarding the method by which it was originally written, for scholars have discussed this very question for the last two centuries without even suggesting that it contains the slightest direct statement concerning its own authorship. The investigation is of the greatest possible importance, and the conclusions which result from it no less so, for this first book of Scripture is the basis on which much of the superstructure, not only of the Old Testament, but also of the New, is reared. Moreover, Genesis has an interest and significance to which no other document of antiquity can aspire.

The proposed solution to the problem of the composition of Genesis outlined in the following pages, is the result of applying the findings which archaeological research has presented to us in recent years. During this period the writer has spent several years in "the land that was Babylonia" (modern south Iraq), visiting the various excavations at the ancient sites, and in constant touch with the latest discoveries. In this environment of ancient things Genesis was carefully reexamined, not for the purpose of discovering a new solution to its composition, but solely to illustrate the geography and archaeology of the country in relation to it.

The Viewpoint Stated

While engaged in these studies the key to its literary composition became increasingly clear, for Genesis was permitted the rare privilege of being allowed to speak for itself in the light of all the knowledge we now possess of the methods of writing practiced in patriarchal times. It would seem that the key to its composition has previously remained unrecognized, and therefore unused. While prevailing theories have been unable to unlock the door to its literary structure, it is submitted that the following explanation does: *The book of Genesis was originally written on tablets in the ancient script of the time by the patriarchs who were intimately concerned with the events related, and whose names are clearly stated. Moreover, Moses, the compiler and editor of the book, as we now have it, plainly directs attention to the source of his information.*

Such a statement needs adequate confirmation by the writer, and on the part of the reader a patient study of all the evidence on which it is based. When this evidence has been scrutinized, the author would claim that it is attested by facts so numerous and verified by undesigned coincidences so overwhelming, that almost every critical difficulty regarding Genesis disappears.

Archaeology and the Earliest Writing

Until the beginning of the last century, the only known contemporary history that had been written earlier than 1000 BC was the early part of the Old Testament. The ancient historical records of Babylonia had not been unearthed but lay buried and unknown beneath mounds and ruins which had hidden them for millenniums. It was because the earlier books of the Bible stood alone and unique in this claim to have been written centuries before any other piece of writing then known to the world, that a century ago critics endeavored to prove they must have been written at a date much later than Moses. On the other hand, the defenders of the Mosaic authorship could not then know that writing was in frequent use a thousand years before he was born. Consequently both sides in the controversy imagined that the contents of Genesis had been handed down by word of mouth, it being assumed that writing was impracticable, and almost unknown in the times of the patriarchs.

P. Ewald was prepared to admit that Moses was acquainted with the art of writing, but he says that "the accounts of the patriarchal time contain no sure traces of the use of writing in that early age." Even as late as 1893, H. Schultz wrote, "of the legendary character of the pre-Mosaic narratives, the time of which they treat is a sufficient proof. It was a time prior to all knowledge of writing" (*Old Testament Theology*).

Constant reference will be made to archaeological research. This is necessary because of the urgent need for a reconsideration of Genesis in the ancient environment in which it came into existence. It will also emancipate us from the prevailing fallacy of investigating the book just as though it should have been written in a manner similar to modern history. It is not possible to avoid reference to the "critical" theories concerning its origin, for while those scholars have sometimes stated clearly certain literary characteristics observable in Genesis, their speculations based on these observations are frequently at variance with the explicit statements of the book itself and also with modern archaeological discoveries. Because the series of conjectures commonly known as "higher criticism" are so widely accepted in certain quarters as an explanation of the method of its composition, it is necessary to test these modern suppositions. It will seem that such conjectures would never have seen the light of day, had scholars of that time been in possession of modern archaeological knowledge. It is therefore submitted that because the critical theories originated in an age of ignorance concerning the earliest patriarchal times, and the newer facts of excavation have rendered them so hopelessly obsolete, the time is overdue for a new appreciation of Genesis in the light of recent archaeological research.

Outline of the Book

For this reason it is necessary to call upon archaeology to be our first witness, to inform us of the facts, and to enlighten us regarding the lessons to be learned from excavation, especially in their bearing on the antiquity of early writing and the literary methods employed. This witness will occupy Chapters 2 to 4 of the first part of this book. Genesis speaks for itself in Chapters 5 to 8. In Chapter 9 reference is made to theories now obsolete. In Chapter 10 Genesis defends itself against attack. In Chapter 11 the titles for God, used in Genesis, are considered. The New Testament use of the ancient narratives and the witness of the Lord Jesus Christ will be discussed in Chapter 12. The evidence is summed up in Chapter 13.

The highest meaning that can be given to the word

"critic" is "a judge." A true judge may not commence his examination of the evidence by taking for granted that the accused book of Genesis is "guilty"; he will listen to the witnesses patiently and impartially. He will be scrupulously fair to weigh the whole of the evidence, and not allow any material fact to be suppressed. Moreover, both sides must be permitted to give their evidence in their own words.

A secondary meaning of the word "critic" is "a hostile witness." The following pages are a plea that the book of Genesis should be given a fair hearing. Because we are in search of the whole truth, the critics in Chapter 9 will put forward their greatest and most eminent advocates and give their witness in their own words—not merely specially selected extracts, but the whole of their material evidence.

It is often easier to be an advocate for the prosecution than for the defense. It is certainly not so difficult to be destructive as constructive, it requires less thought to pull down than to build up. One match can be used to fire a palace which will take many men a considerable time to replace. It is not difficult to suggest doubt or suspicion against a book, but it may take much time and labor to clear it of the charges and restore it to confidence. It is intended that these pages should be constructive.

II

Discoveries in Babylonia

The discoveries in Babylonia which have aroused the greatest interest among the general public have been those connected with the Bible. In the early days of excavation, the finding of a palace belonging to a king mentioned in Scripture, or of an inscription referring to an Old Testament incident, produced not merely excitement but sensation. To this day the excavations at Ur of the Chaldees have been followed with far greater interest by the majority than the unearthing of the older city of Kish; simply because Abraham may well have lived at Ur, and from it journeyed to Palestine, while Kish, having no direct connection with the Bible, is not of great interest except to archaeologists.

It was not until the middle of the last century that excavators began digging among the ruined mounds of Mesopotamia. Just a few decades ago these long undulating hills of earth were the undisturbed grave clothes covering the remains of the oldest civilizations. The Arab pitched his black goats' hair tent on these hills, and with unseeing eyes followed his primitive plow as it was dragged around these mounds of earth. This was all that was then visible of Babylon, Ur, Erech, and Calneh in the land of Shinar; and Asshur, Nineveh and Calah in the land of Asshur. The sands of time had covered these cities so thoroughly that less than a hundred years ago they appeared to be merely ordinary hills. Except for their elevation they seemed to be composed of nothing but the dust of the desert. However, rain storms had partially furrowed their sides, revealing pieces of broken pottery and tablets on which had been imprinted an intricate pattern made up of combinations of wedge-shaped indentations, referred to as "cuneiform."

In Egypt, the great monuments—the pyramids, temples and palaces—had at least kept their heads above the shifting sands of the desert, thus partially remaining visible to the wondering gaze of men. But in Mesopotamia the cities were so thoroughly buried, that it had become a land of dead cities; moreover, so obliterated had the places of their internment become that their sites were either unknown or uncertain. The mounds masked their secrets so well that with few exceptions the inhabitants of the country knew no more of what lay beneath them than did the sheep who fed on their scanty spring grass. Now jackals and scorpions make their homes in their ruins, "her cities are a desolation, dry land and a wilderness" (Jer. 51:43). Even today there are many mounds of which we know nothing, either of their past or present contents. Quite recently some distinguished archaeologists who had not only repeatedly visited a certain ancient site but who had thoroughly surveyed it, passed it by unrecognized more than once, supposing it to be an unknown ruin.

The Mounds in Babylonia

It is necessary to restrict this brief review of excavation to the lands referred to in the earlier chapters of the book of Genesis; the lands of Shinar and Asshur, until lately known as Mesopotamia (the land between the rivers) but now called Iraq. In early times the southern part of the country was known as Babylonia and the northern as Assyria. Still earlier, the southern plain was called Sumer and the more northerly Agade (Accad). This country is a strip of land, some 600 miles long and 250 miles broad, now extending from the Kurdish mountains in the north to the Persian Gulf in the south, with the Persian or Iranian mountains as its eastern border and on its western, the desert of Arabia. It is a land uniform in its flatness, down which the two great rivers, the Tigris and Euphrates, flow.

Here civilization commenced; here excavators have discovered the beginnings of history, and out of its soil the most ancient forms of writing have been dug. It is the cradle of the human race.

It is not surprising that early travelers mistook the buried cities for ordinary hills. So obliterated were the ruins of the city of Bablyon, that it is questionable whether some of those who wrote about the great city knew exactly where it was, for they describe mounds quite different in shape and size to those of the ruins of Babylon. Benjamin of Tudela, a Spanish Jew, who visited the country in the twelfth century, writing of these ruins, says that they were "to men inaccessible on account of the various and malignant kinds of serpents and scorpions living there" (*Itenerarium*), while Marco Polo seems to have passed them by unnoticed. On the other hand the site of Babylon appears to have been known to the Arabs, for De Beauchamp, who visited it twice between 1780 and 1790, says of the ruins that "they are exactly under the mound the Arabs call Babel."

Sir Antony Shirley, who traveled through Mesopotamia at the end of the sixteenth century, wrote of "Nineve, that which God Himself called That great Citie, hath not one stone standing which may give memory of the being of a town." Tavernier visited Mosul in

1644, and referring to these ruins said, "They appear a formless mass of ruined houses extending almost a mile alongside the river. One recognises there a large number of vaults or holes which are all uninhabited."

Early Attempts at Solution

The first attempt to solve the mystery of the contents of these mounds was made at the beginning of the last century, but it was not until 1842 that the work of excavation properly commenced. Even then, little effort was made to obtain written records because excavators could not read them, and the few scholars engaged upon the task had not themselves entirely solved the puzzle of cuneiform writing. It must be admitted that in those early days excavators were searching mainly for sculpture which would adorn the museums of London and Paris.

Claudius James Rich may be called the first excavator. His ability to acquire oriental languages had become evident quite early; so much so, that at the age of sixteen he was appointed to a military cadetship in the East India Company's service. At twenty-one he became the Company's resident at Baghdad. Thereafter all the time he could spare from his official duties he devoted to his historical researches. He visited Babylon in December of 1811 and wrote about the desolation and confusion that existed there, and of the brick robbers who had been carrying away Nebuchadnezzar's bricks for ordinary building purposes. The East India Company requested him to send home specimens of these bricks and the clay tablets inscribed with wedge writing. These were forwarded in a box three feet square. At that time a small glass case in the British Museum contained all that Britain possessed of the antiquities of Babylonia. In 1821, aged 34, Rich died of cholera.

The remaining mounds, covering the numerous cities of ancient days, were left undisturbed until 1842 when France sent Paul Emil Botta to Mosul as their Consul. On the eastern bank of the Tigris, opposite Mosul, lay the ruins of Nineveh; two mounds of which were prominent. He expected the southern tell, called Nebi Yunus (i.e. Prophet Jonah) to yield the best results, but on the summit of this mound was a small village including a mosque which the Arabs claimed to contain the tomb of the prophet Jonah. Here Botta found that the owners of the houses and land either refused him permission to dig or requested far greater sums for the privilege than he was prepared to pay. He was therefore restricted to the northern mound known as Kouyunjik, but success did not attend his excavations. However, early in the proceedings a peasant from the village of Khorsabad, some thirty miles north of Nineveh, happening to pass the diggings and finding that Botta was in search of stones with pictures on them, volunteered the information that in his village there were plenty of such stones. The Frenchman, having already learned the tendency of the Arab to wish to be the bearer of good news, took little notice of the peasant's story; but having had months of unsuccessful digging at Nineveh, he sent some of his workmen to the Arab's village to see what they could find. As soon as digging began they came across sculptured bas-reliefs and inscriptions. An Assyrian palace had been found. When the news of this discovery reached Paris it created such interest that funds were immediately placed at Botta's disposal to continue the work. By 1844 numerous rooms in the palace had been unearthed, and it was identified as the palace of Sargon II, who is mentioned in Isaiah 20:1 as sending his general against Ashdod. Botta also discovered a magnificent alabaster wall sculpture of Sargon accompanied by his general.

In 1851, Victor Place succeeded Botta, not only as the French Consulate at Mosul but also as excavator of Khorsabad. He spent the next four years in unearthing the palace of Sargon. Apart from the reference to Sargon in Isaiah, practically nothing was known of this monarch. Now the rooms in which he had lived, and sculptured representations of him that had been lost to sight for 2,500 years, became familiar. Monsieur Place put sixty-eight cases containing some of these great sculptures and inscriptions, together with those he had collected from Babylon, on a raft and sent them down the Tigris for shipment to Paris. But before the raft reached the junction of the Euphrates and the Tigris, it foundered with all its precious cargo.

Early British Initiatives

It was not long before Great Britain became represented in northern or Assyrian archaeology in the person of Austen Henry Layard. From early years he had an enthusiasm for the East, yet had been contracted with a solicitor in London. After six years in the office he abandoned law and went to Constantinople, where he hoped to obtain an appointment as attaché at the British Embassy. In 1839 he commenced touring the Near East—in those days a long and perilous undertaking. On his way to Persia in 1840 he visited Mosul, and on the return in 1842 he met Botta at Nineveh. In 1845 Sir Stratford Canning, the Ambassador at Constantinople, instead of making him the attache, gave him fifty pounds for archaeological research. This, together with his own money, enabled him to realize the aspirations of the last five years. He set off at once for Mosul, and in order to attract as little attention as possible, said nothing whatever to anyone about his plans. With only six workmen, he went twenty-five miles down the eastern bank of the

Tigris to a mound called Nimrud—the Calah of Genesis 10. On the first day he discovered an Assyrian palace, on the third he came across numerous fragments of cuneiform tablets, but for the latter he was not searching, for he could not decipher this cuneiform writing.

One day when he was away from the excavations Layard saw two mounted Arabs riding towards him at top speed. On reaching him one excitedly exclaimed, "Hasten, O Bey, hasten to the diggers, for they have found Nimrod himself!—*Wallah* it is wonderful but it is true, we have seen him with our own eyes." They had discovered one of the great human-headed, winged lions now in the British Museum. Scarcely a day passed without unearthing something of value, but on one occasion when he had dug a fifty-foot trench into one of the mounds, he was about to abandon it because nothing worthwhile had been traced, when a workman unearthed a black marble monument—the now famous obelisk of Shalmaneser III—inscribed on which are the words, "I received the tribute of Jehu Son of Omri silver and gold," etc. When Colonel Rawlinson at Baghdad deciphered this inscription referring to the king of Israel, the news of the "find" created a considerable impression. Layard commanded a second expedition in 1849-51 and the results were so good that it required hundreds of cases to send even part of the acquired treasure to the British Museum.

Discovery of a Great Library

Hormuzd Rassam, a resident of Mosul who had assisted Layard, took charge of the operations two years later. At first he found little to encourage him at Nimrud, so he turned his attention to the mound Kouyunjik at Nineveh. Here he found the palace of Ashurbanipal, and on the sides of one room was a bas-relief depicting the king standing in his hunting chariot, with his servants around him handing him the weapons for the chase. More important still, he found the great king's immense library containing tens of thousands of tablets, but unfortunately many of them were either broken or burnt. Ashurbanipal was a great collector of ancient tablets—he boasted of his ambitions in this respect—and was known to have sent scribes to distant cities to reproduce their most important tablets, some of which were quite ancient even then. The tablets found by Rassam were packed in the primitive fashion of those days and shipped to the British Museum, where, owing to the fact that they were so numerous and the decipherers so few, they remained in the cellars for many years before it was discovered that among them were the king's copies of the Babylonian Creation and Flood tablets. These were recognized nearly twenty years afterwards by George Smith and immediately became famous.

During all this time Babylonia had been almost ignored, excavators having concentrated their attention on the northern mounds of Assyria. In 1849 Colonel Rawlinson, and in 1854 J. E. Taylor, visited Ur of the Chaldees, while in the latter year Rawlinson made researches both at Babylon and at Birs Nimrod. During these years Loftus surveyed these and other sites, but owing to the threatening attitude of the southern Arab, could not excavate them. In 1878 Rassam dug trenches into the mounds of Babylon, securing some important inscriptions, but none so spectacular were found there as those yielded by the mounds of Assyria. Excavators, therefore, again turned their attention to Nineveh.

Finds at Nineveh

George Smith, who commenced his career at the British Museum as an engraver, unremittingly surmounted the difficulties in the translation of cuneiform writing, until he became one of the most skillful decipherers of his day. In the course of his work at the Museum he recognized and deciphered the Flood tablets (which had been discovered nearly twenty years before), and disclosed his find to the world in a paper read before the Society of Biblical Archaeology in December 1872. Such was the intense interest it created, that in 1873 the *Daily Telegraph* gave one thousand pounds to defray the cost of Smith going to Nineveh to search for the missing portions of these tablets and for additional exploration. At Nineveh, he was cleaning the dust from some tablets when he sighted some of the missing lines. He returned to England but set out again in November of the same year on a second expedition, for the permission granted by the Turkish authorities to excavate was to lapse in four months. Notwithstanding considerable difficulties he worked rapidly, unearthing numerous inscribed clay tablets, and on his return gave his attention to those that would illustrate the Old Testament, particularly the earlier chapters of Genesis. In March 1876, we find him again leaving for Nineveh, but on his arrival in the country he found cholera so prevalent that it was impossible to commence excavations. Forgetful of the climatic dangers of this country, exposed to the terrific heat of the midday sun, often without food, and even in these conditions, overexerting himself, he left Nineveh for London a disappointed man, because on this occasion he had accomplished nothing. He got no further than Aleppo, where on the 19th of August, 1876, he died. George Smith was one of the most successful Assyriologists that Britain has known.

It was not until 1888 that America began to take a direct and active part in Babylonian excavation. In that year they commenced work on the mound which the Arabs called Nippur, and excavations there were most determinedly carried out, in spite of considerable opposition, until World War I. From this mound thousands of tablets were obtained, and the texts which have been published, some in more recent years, reveal many of great importance.

However, it is only in the last few years that excavation has reached back to the times outlined in the early chapters of Genesis. The discoveries in Assyria and Babylonia during the last century rarely took us back beyond the age of Moses.

At the dawn of the twentieth century, the discovery of the Code of Hammurabi placed us in possession of the laws prevalent in the days of Abraham. Concerning the centuries before this, archaeology was dim and uncertain. The researches of recent years have, however, brought to light a number of astounding and valuable facts relating to the times covered by Genesis.

Finds at Ur

In 1922 Mr. (later, Sir Leonard) Woolley of the British Museum, acting in cooperation with the University of Pennsylvania, commenced the systematic excavation of Ur of the Chaldees. From the very beginning of the work, this expert archaeologist demonstrated beyond a shadow of doubt the high state of civilization existing in early times. Yet in 1923, when I watched his workmen in the process of removing thousands of tons of earth in order to reveal the great ziggurat or "high place," built 250 years before Abraham was born, I scarcely realized that the later results of this expedition would yield such rich treasures and throw so great a flood of light on the times of Genesis. This "high place" is the best preserved specimen in the whole of the country; it is a solid mass of brickwork 200 feet long, 150 feet wide and originally about 75 feet high. During this excavation some bricks with the inscription of Ur-Nammu, the builder of this temple tower, were found. One of these was given to me, and on it the cuneiform characters are perfectly stamped, thus revealing that writing was common hundreds of years before the time of Abraham.

A year later I was shown a tablet which had just been found at Al Ubaid, some four miles from Ur. It belonged to the period of 5,000 years ago and was one of the most ancient specimens of writing then known. C. J. Gadd, of the British Museum, who that season was at Ur, had found on it the names of two Sumerian rulers, one of whom was known but the other up to the moment of the discovery had been regarded even by archaeologists to be quite legendary. It certainly adds to the reality of the background of Genesis, to watch, as I did, the excavation of the wall with which Ur-Nammu encircled his city two centuries before Abraham lived there. This wall was seventy-seven feet thick and three miles round.

In 1929 Sir Leonard Woolley instructed his workmen to dig a deep pit in a selected part of the city. In doing this they unexpectedly found a remarkable change in the character of the soil, for clean water-laid clay suddenly commenced. The Arab workmen reported it and were told to continue digging down. After a depth of eight feet this clean water-laid clay eased as suddenly as it had commenced, for below it broken pottery was found and other evidences of the existence of a village before the layer of clay became deposited. The place where this discovery occurred was down through strata which covered the sloping face of a mound, and the thickness of the water-laid clay varied across it from eight to eleven feet in depth. The water necessary to lay such a great thickness

of deposit must have been so considere'
Leonard Wooley came to the conclusion thaᴜ
possible explanation of his discovery was that theᵧ
found definite evidence of the effects of the Flood. In tnᴜ
season 1929-30 he dug down through the Flood level into
virgin soil, and in 1934 he sank another pit some distance away, again through the water-laid clay of the
Flood, discovering some statues and pottery in the pre-
Flood level. At the conclusion of this last season's work,
he told me that his findings regarding the Flood had
been abundantly confirmed. I have examined this Flood
earth. The complete absence of salt prevalent in other
levels, its exceptional nature, the sudden beginning and
as abrupt cessation, then the recommencement of broken pottery and bones beneath it, are certainly most remarkable evidence of a Flood.[1]

Beginning in the year 1927, at a level which he later
dated 3500 BC, Sir Leonard Woolley unearthed a large
cemetery, and many grim discoveries suggested deaths
which had probably been violent. In it, however, were
many fine examples of the type of golden headdress
worn by women of those times, also numerous bead
necklaces. One of the most spectacular finds was that of
a golden helmet of Mes-kalam-dug, whom Sir Leonard
placed as having lived about 3500 BC.[2]

At Kish and Nippur

Professor S. H. Langdon commenced researches at
Kish and Jemdat Nasr in 1923, which have been exceedingly fruitful in their contribution to our knowledge of

---

[1] Published by the British Museum, *Ur Excavations*, 4 (1956); Sir. C. L.
Wooley. Cf. also M. E. L Mallowan, "Noah's Flood Reconsidered," *Iraq*
26 (1964), pp. 62-82.
[2] Now dated *ca.* 2650 BC.

the earliest periods of civilization. I was at Kish two days after the discovery of a stone tablet in a semi-pictographic script, believed to be one of the oldest pieces of writing known to man. Here also, a distance of 150 miles from Ur, evidence of the Flood was found.

At Nippur the expedition of the University of Pennsylvania found a large number of inscriptions dating before the time of Abraham; these have been published by the University Press. In the volume issued in 1914 by Dr. Arno Poebel (*Historical Texts*), he reproduces a series of tablets relating to the Creation and the Flood, and "ten rulers who reigned before the Flood." It is quite possible that the latter corresponds to the ten patriarchs mentioned in Genesis 5. These tablets are written in one of the earliest forms of cuneiform script known.

Later, Mr. H. Weld-Blundell obtained a number of inscribed clay prisms which had been found at Larsa. These he has presented to the Ashmolean Museum at Oxford, and Professor S. H. Langdon studied and deciphered them. One known as WB 444 contains a complete list of men who "ruled before the Flood"; the names are then given of those who ruled "after the Flood" until the year 2000 BC. Another (WB 62) gives a list of ten persons who "ruled before the Flood."

Signs of Early Development

Reference should also be made to Dr. H. H. Frankfort's *Third Preliminary Report on the Excavations at Tell Asmar (Eshunna)*. Under the chapter heading of "The Religion of Eshunna in the Third Millennium BC," he writes:

> In addition to their more tangible results, our excavations have established a novel fact, which the student of Babylonian religions will have henceforth to take into account. We have obtained, to the best of our knowledge

for the first time, religious material complete in its social setting. We possess a coherent mass of evidence, derived in almost equal quantity from a temple and from the houses inhabited by those who worshipped in that temple. We are thus able to draw conclusions which the finds studied by themselves would not have made possible. For instance, we discover that the representation on cylinder seals, which are usually connected with various gods, can all be fitted in to form a consistent picture in which a single god worshipped in this temple forms the central figure. It seems, therefore, that at this early period his various aspects were not considered separate deities in the Sumero-Akkadian pantheon.

This illuminating statement throws light on the way polytheism developed from monotheism; it used to be imagined that the reverse was the case.

Warka (the Erech of Genesis 10) has been partially excavated by German archaeologists who found remarkable evidence of an advanced state of civilization in pre-Abrahamic days.

During subsequent years excavators have been busy tracing the various strata of civilizations backwards into the very twilight of history.

The Background of the Patriarchal Age

Many of the sites excavated in the last seventy years go back to the days of Genesis, for it is with the earliest civilizations that archaeologists are now concerned. They have brought to light the culture and writing of men who lived 5,000 years ago; their investigations have reached even to pre-Flood days. These researches have revolutionized thought, for concerning the civilizations of this early period we previously had known next to nothing. They have done more, for they have painted in the background on a canvas which previously was almost blank. We now understand much concerning the environment of the patriarchs and the methods of writing prevalent in the times of Genesis. Before these excavations this early period was considered legendary even by archaeologists, but almost beyond their highest hopes they have been able to grid and plan settlements which were previously in the realm of pre-history. Now, in the opinion of these experienced men, Sumerian civilization had reached its zenith centuries before Abraham.

The archaeologists are by no means engaged in an attempt to find evidences which agree with the Bible. I know from personal contact and repeated discussions that this is far from being their aim. They sift their evidence in a most critical spirit and, if there is any bias, it is in favor of the critical standpoint rather than that of the Bible. Yet, in the words of more than one, they have expressed the truth of the matter when they have affirmed that they have been compelled by the evidence they have unearthed to accept that Genesis in this or that respect is accurate. It has been my privilege to have been present with the excavators when some of these evidences were unearthed. I have been impressed with the tremendous change which has taken place in their outlook on these early biblical records, and the assurance with which they now speak of events recorded in Genesis.

III

Evidence of
Advanced Civilizations

No more surprising fact has been discovered by recent excavation than the suddenness with which civilization appeared in the world. This discovery is the very opposite to that anticipated. It was expected that the more ancient the period, the more primitive would excavators find it to be, until traces of civilization ceased altogether and aboriginal man appeared. Neither in Babylonia nor Egypt, the lands of the oldest known habitations of man, has this been the case. In this connection, Dr. H. R. Hall writes in his *History of the Near East*, "When civilisation appears it is already full grown," and again, "Sumerian culture springs into view ready made." And Dr. L. W. King in *Sumer and Akkad*, says, "Although the earliest Sumerian settlements in southern Babylonia are to be set back in a comparatively remote past, the race by which they were founded appears at that time to have already attained to a high level of culture."

All the real evidence we have, that of Genesis, archaeology, and the traditions of men, points to the Mesopotamian plain as the oldest home of man. Far Eastern civilization, whether Chinese or Indian, cannot compete with this land in the antiquity of its peoples, for it can easily sustain its claim to be the cradle of civilization. Yet, notwithstanding this, it is not possible to push back the habitation of man in this land many millenniums into the past, for the very simple and conclusive reason that the more southern Mesopotamian land must have been formed within the last 10,000 years or so. We know that owing to the peculiar nature of the rivers in bringing down silt and depositing it at the entrance to the Persian Gulf, the land has been formed gradually during the past millenniums; the land is still being added to by this means. Ur of the Chaldees, which was once on the edge of the Persian Gulf, is now over one hundred miles from it.[1]

Advanced Civilizations

In some of these southern sites, in places where it is known that earliest man inhabited, archaeologists have, as we have seen, dug down to the virgin soil. They are dealing with these earliest traces of civilization of the period 3500-2500 BC. Writing about the era of 3500 BC, Sir Leonard Woolley says in *The Sumerians*:

> It is astonishing to find that at this early period the Sumerians were acquainted with and commonly employed not only the column, but the arch, the vault and (as may be argued from the apsidal ends of the chambers) the dome, architectural forms which were not to find their way into the western world for thousands of years. That the general level of civilisation accorded with the high development of architecture is shown by the richness of the graves. Objects of gold and silver are abundant, not only personal ornaments but vessels,

---

[1] This has been discussed most recently by C. F. Larsen, "The Mesopotamia Delta Region," *Journal of American Oriental Society*, 95 (1975), pp. 43-57.

weapons and even tools being made of the precious metals: copper is the metal of everyday use.

In his report on the "Technical achievements of the third millennium BC as evidenced at Tell Asmar," Dr. H. H. Frankfort writes, "Man's mastery over matter progressed further in early dynastic and Akkadian times than is often believed, and it will be useful to discuss here briefly a few relevant discoveries." He then cites the use of glass at 2600-2700 BC and also the analysis made by C. H. Desch of the National Physical Laboratory, London, of some bronze objects found at Ur containing a quantity of tin "corresponding to a true casting bronze." At Tell Asmar the majority of metal objects were made of copper, but Dr. Frankfort continues, "with us the bronze of a knife handle remains an isolated instance. A knife blade from one of the private houses, however, contains 2.8 per cent of tin." He also writes of "a most unexpected discovery made during the last season, that iron was used for tools before 2700 BC—more than fifteen hundred years before the day when the first iron dagger known was sent, presumably by a Hittite king, as a present to the youthful Tutenkhamen of Egypt." The bone of the handles found at Tell Asmar had gone, but the silver foil that had covered them remained.

Sir Leonard Woolley, who had done so much to illuminate the period before Abraham, writes in *The Sumerians*:

About 2000 BC, after the fall of the Third Dynasty at Ur, Sumerian scribes took it in hand to record the glories of the great days that had passed away. They must have had at their disposal a mass of documentary evidence, and from this they compiled, on the one hand the political history, and on the other hand the religious traditions of the land. Their histories have perished, or survive only in excerpts embodied in Babylonian chronicles of a much later date.

The Peak Period of Development

It was confidently expected that excavation would support the widely held view of a gradual development of civilization. But the cumulative evidence to the contrary has grown to such substantial proportions in those two countries, Iraq and Egypt, where we find the most ancient civilizations, that it seems that soon after the Flood, civilization reached a peak from which it was to recede. Instead of the infinitely slow development anticipated, it has become obvious that art, and we may say science, suddenly burst upon the world. For instance, in his *Outline of History*, H. G. Wells suggests that the oldest stone building known to the world is the Saqqara Pyramid. Yet, as Dr. J. H. Breasted points out in his *Conquest of Civilization*, "from the earliest piece of stone masonry to the construction of the great Pyramid, less than a century and a half elapsed."

Writing of this step pyramid, Sir Flinders Petrie states:

> The accuracy of construction is evidence of high purpose and great capability and training. In the earliest pyramid the precision of the whole mass is such that the error would be exceeded by that of a metal measure used on a mild or a cold day; the error of levelling is less than can be seen with the naked eye....The conclusion seems inevitable that at 3000 BC was the heyday of Egyptian art.

The first stone building erected at Saqqara as the funerary temple of King Zoser was excavated by Mr. C. M. Firth for the Egyptian Government. Of it, Dr. H. R. Hall of the British Museum writes:

> This building is of extraordinary interest, as the first fruits of the young Egyptian genius in the field of architecture. In it we see features such as the columns and the decoration, that it is difficult to believe can be so old as

the IIIrd dynasty; but there are others that are obviously archaic....It is easy to say that this remarkable outburst of architectural capacity must argue a long previous apprenticeship and period of development; but in this case we have not got this long period. The Egyptians of the first dynasty, some three centuries before, had apparently no stone buildings, and the reign of Zoser was in later legend notable because he had built the first stone house.

Even this rapid development was to be outdistanced, for within a period of 150 years after the erection of this first stone building, the mightiest building in stone the world has ever known had been achieved. Khufu, or Cheops as the Greeks named him, called the great pyramid "the Glorious." It was about 480 feet high, and covered 12 1/2 acres; notwithstanding the number of stones which have been removed, it still contains 85,000,000 cubic feet of masonry. Herodotus says that it took ten years to quarry the stone and another ten years to build it into the pyramid. According to Diodorus, 300,000 men were employed on the work. All this expenditure of time and labor, in the words of the "British Museum Guide" on Egypt, was in order to reproduce "the most magnificent tomb in the world as his last resting place." It must be remembered that this swift progress in architecture was not maintained. Sir Flinders Petrie says: "The materials used in building tell much about the builders. In the series of pyramids the finest material and work is at the beginning, and through the IVth to the VIth dynasties the degeneration is continuous, until a pyramid was a mere shell of building filled with chips." This sudden burst of achievement, which occurred in Babylonia at the same period, made a lasting impression on the architecture of these countries.

It is not merely the massiveness of the great pyramid that impresses; in its construction the building reveals a greater knowledge of astronomy than was prevalent in civilized Europe 3,500 years later. Art, and we may say science, had already triumphed. The Sphinx, a statue of the second pyramid builder, is in the form of a king's head with a lion's body; the body is 187 feet long and the head 66 feet high. The man who planned the pyramid and had the stones cut with such finesse that they fit with marvelous perfection, who organized the transportation of these millions of tons of stone to the site and their elevation to such heights, was not in a primitive state with a pigmy brain, even though only 150 years had elapsed since the first stone building had been erected.

Slow Progress of Man Disproved

In the face of these facts, the slow progress of early man is a disproved assumption, and the idea that an infinitely prolonged period elapsed before civilization appeared cannot be maintained. The prevailing theory in this respect is most assertive where it has least evidence.

Four thousand years ago in Babylonia, men were highly developed in certain arts and technical trades. For instance, two bronze goats' heads made in this period, when analyzed, were found to be made of 82.9 per cent copper, 1.33 per cent nickel, 0.88 per cent iron, 0.23 per cent antimony, and 14.61 per cent oxygen. A silver vase was found in Telloh, in circumstances which the excavators say indicate it to be nearly 4,500 years old. On it is the coat-of-arms of Lagash (four eagles with outstretched wings), also representations of stags and lions; it is a remarkable and skillful piece of work. Their lapidary work was never excelled in subsequent times and can scarcely be surpassed in some respects in the present day, even with all our modern implements and improvements. The pottery of the Sumerian age, the early civilization of Babylonia, is more expertly made than at any later period. Archaeologists have taken us into the distant past and still they find civilization at a high state of culture. In the words of Sir Leonard Woolley (*The Sumerians*), "so far as we know, the fourth millennium before Christ saw Sumerian art at its zenith."

These Sumerians claim to be the earliest inhabitants of the country. In his *History and Monuments of Ur*, C. J. Gadd writes:

> The Sumerians possessed the land since as far back in time as anything at all is seen or even obscurely divined, and it has already been remarked that their own legends, which profess to go back to the creation of the world and of men, have their setting in no other land than their historical home....But the shapes of the flints are not those of a pure stone age, nor has any certain evidence yet been found in Iraq of a population so primitive as to have no knowledge of metal.

This recalls the words of Berosus who, writing in the third century BC, says that these southern Mesopotamian people introduced into the world the method of using metal and the art of writing; "in a word all the things that make for the betterment of life were bequeathed to men by Oannes, and since that time no further inventions have been made." Writing of the first historical age in Babylonia, Dr. Gadd adds:

> Words of art which astonish by their beauty have been found, not least at Ur itself, to be the relics of the first, not the last ages. Nothing but the good fortune that they were recovered by regular excavation could have avoided a ludicrous misconception of their date....Gold is the material of their possessions and the symbol of their superfluity. In their flourishing days and at their lavish court, the arts of manufacture rose to a perfection and beauty in their products which was never seen again. The articles made were indeed of much the same kind as

those of later ages, but they were, at this very early period, marked by a richness and splendour rather of Egyptian sumptuosity than the supposed sobriety of the River-lands. These deposits amaze by their riot of gold; silver also is there in great profusion, evidently nothing accounted of.

Neither the Bible nor Babylonian excavation know anything of uncivilized man. Life at the beginning was necessarily simple, but it seems that it was not only enlightened, it was cultured.

IV

Methods of the Scribes in 3000 BC

One of the most remarkable facts which has emerged from archaeological research, is that the art of writing began in the earliest historical times known to man. It is now generally agreed that history first dawned in the land known as Babylonia, and that civilization there is older than that of Egypt. Both civilizations are characterized by the use of written records. Until recent times it was the general tendency to insist on the late appearance of writing. Now the pendulum has swung to the opposite direction, and the present tendency is to thrust back the period for which written records are claimed to about 3500 BC. Egyptologists have discovered documents written on papyrus which they claim may be dated as early as 3000 BC.

When visiting Professor Langdon of Oxford University, who was excavating at Kish, I witnessed the unearthing of what is believed to be the oldest piece of writing ever found. It was on a stone tablet and in the form of line pictures. This "line picture writing" is thought by many to be a development of a still older form of writing by which the ancients made ordinary pictures convey their thoughts on stone or clay. This infant system of writing while decidedly primitive is by no means crude, for the Egyptians used it at the height of their art and power. Such a method of conveying ideas through pictures has been revived recently; it is used for wayside signs, by picture newspapers and illustrated advertisements. Some of the ancient forms of picture writing are so old that they cannot now be deciphered; when, however, such picture writing as that of the Egyptian hieroglyphics is used, it conveys the thoughts of the writers intelligibly and accurately.

A conservative estimate is that the pictographic forms of writing which have been found may be dated from 3300 to 2800 BC; thereafter cuneiform writing came into use.

Writing and Writing Materials

In the very early days clay became the common material on which to write, though stone was used in some instances. The clay of the Euphrates valley is remarkable for its fineness; it is as fine as well-ground flour. When made plastic with water it was shaped into the size desired to be written upon and the writing done with a stylus made of metal or wood, one end of which was triangular. This stylus was held in the palm of the hand, and a corner of it was pressed into the plastic clay, leaving a mark which resembled a wedge (hence cuneiform writing, from *cuneus*, a wedge). All the signs were made up of single wedges, placed parallel, at various angles, or across each other. By this means nearly 600 entirely independent and distinct signs were made by use of from one to thirty wedges. There were many scribes and, though the sizes of the stylus used and consequently that of the wedges varied, yet the general character of the script remained much the same in each period of history. The care and neatness bestowed upon a tablet is often indicative of its importance.

After this wedge writing had been impressed on the soft clay, the tablet was either dried in the great heat of the Babylonian sun or baked in a special kiln. The scribes mixed a little chalk or gypsum with the clay, because they found that by doing so, when the tablet dried, it scarcely shrank and did not crack. *These clay tablets are, next to stone, the most imperishable form of writing material known to man.* Even when dried in the sun they become so hard that for thousands of years they have remained intact and legible. Great care is however necessary when excavating sun-dried tablets if damp earth has come into contact with them. But after they have been dried, they again become so hard that it is difficult to tell they were not baked in a kiln.

As early as 2350 BC clay envelopes were used for private letters and contract tablets, and it became the practice to rewrite the contents of the tablet on the envelope, then to close it with a private seal. The owner could be assured that the contents had not been tampered with if the seal remained intact. Should a dispute arise the tablet within was examined.

It is probable, then, that from earliest times, the thoughts of men were set down in writing by the use of pictures or signs. These developed into "line pictures" because straight lines were more easily inscribed on such substances as stone and clay. When clay became the common writing material, a series of wedges were impressed on the plastic clay so as to form pictures. At length pictures were almost entirely abandoned and groups of wedges formed words. Of some early Sumerian tablets found at Telloh, Professor L. W. King wrote, "these documents from the nature of their clay and the beauty of their writing are among the finest specimens yet discovered in Babylonia" (*Sumer and Akkad*).

Flourishing Cuneiform Correspondence

Cuneiform writing must have become general at an early date. Thousands of clay tablets have been found written before the patriarchal age. Altogether there are more than a quarter of a million cuneiform clay tablets distributed among the various museums of the world. So common did writing become in Babylonia that a German scholar, Friedrich Delitzsch, wrote:

> In truth, when we find among the letters which have survived from those ancient times in great abundance, the letter of a woman to her husband in his travels, wherein after telling him that the little ones are well, she asks advice on some trivial matter; or the missive of a son to his father, in which he informs him that so-and-so has mortally offended him, that he would thrash the knave, but would like to ask his father's advice first; or another letter in which a son urges his father to send at last the long-promised money, offering the insolent inducement that then he will pray for his father again—all this points to a well-organised system of communication by letter and of postal arrangements.

The following is a typical letter written for Hammurabi, once thought to be identified with the Amraphel who was chased by Abraham as recorded in Genesis 14. It is about a tax collector named Shep-Sin who had been making excuses for not remitting to the treasury the fee which he had agreed to pay for the right of collecting the taxes in a country district of Babylonia.

> Concerning chief collector Shep-Sin I have written to thee: "Send him with the 1800 gur of sesame and 19 minae of silver owed by him as well as chief collector Sin-Mushtal with the 1800 gur of sesame and 7 minae of silver owed by him, send them to Babylon." But thou last replied that the chief collector had said: "Lo it is harvest-time. After the harvest we will go." Thus they have said

and thou hast informed me. Now the harvest is over. So soon as thou seest this tablet which I address to thee, send to Babylon Shep-Sin, the chief collector with the 1800 gur of sesame and 19 minae of silver owed by him; with them thy loyal guard. And let them come to present themselves before me with all their wealth (*The Letters and Inscriptions of Hammurabi*, translated by L. W. King).

Nearly a thousand years before Abraham was born and a millennium and a half before the birth of Moses, Lugalzaggisi, King of Erech, began his inscriptions with words which do not differ greatly from those used by the last king of Babylon, 2,200 years later. To quote L. Delaport:

> Schools existed where lessons were given in reading, and in tracing on clay the elements of the script's signs. That of Nippur was, in the first millennium, the most famous for the antiquity of the texts preserved in its archives. A number of tablets from the century of Hammurabi, as well as models and copies, illustrate the methods of instruction—first reading and writing simple signs with a study of their various phonetic values; then the pupil's initiation into the use consecutively of groups of signs and ideograms, and then of current formulae. He was next given instructions in grammar in the guise of paradigms—declensions and conjugations. Finally he finished his education with mathematics.[1]

One other quotation (from the Preface of D. D. Luckenbill's *Ancient Records of Assyria and Babylonia*) must suffice. "This writing material was cheap, which may account in part for the fact that the Sumerians, Babyloni-

---

[1] This has been confirmed by studies in the education of a scribe; e.g., S. N. Kramer, *Schooldays* (1949); C. J. Gadd, *Teachers and Students in the Oldest Schools* (1956).

ans and Assyrians seemed unwilling to transact even the smallest items of business without recourse to a written document."

In Egypt, where the papyrus plant flourished, papyrus became the usual material on which to write. The earliest papyrus manuscript still in existence is stated to have been written about 3000 BC. The papyrus rolls, written upon with pen and ink, were usually nine to ten inches wide, and one example is 144 feet long. Papyrus as a writing material does not appear to have been used to any extent in Iraq; the inscribed clay tablet, baked hard, was considered a more appropriate and endurable substance for that country.

The cuneiform system of writing became general in all the civilized countries east of the Mediterranean; it was also adopted by the Hittites who are so often mentioned in Genesis. That it was understood in Egypt is evident from the Tell-el-Amarna tablets, of which some 300 were found in that country in 1887. Among them we find letters dated about 1400 BC from Palestine officials to the Egyptian government, all written in cuneiform.

We are by no means certain exactly when Hebrew was introduced into Palestine. Until recently the earliest examples of the Phoenician script, on which Hebrew characters are based, were the Moabite Stone (850 BC) and the Siloam inscription (700 BC). However, since 1930 discoveries have been made at Ras Shamra in Syria, of a library of tablets written in cuneiform. In many of these a few wedge signs are used as an alphabet, thus taking this type of script back to 1300 BC. It is to excavations in Syria and Palestine that we must look for light on the problem of the origin of Hebrew. Akkadian (Babylonian and Assyrian) is as close to Hebrew as any other language and many words are common to both languages.

Deciphering the Cuneiform

We must now turn to the story of the early attempts to decipher cuneiform writing; only a brief outline can be given here for it is a long and intricate one. When specimens of cuneiform writing first were brought to Europe, scholars even doubted whether it was real writing, thinking it merely a form of oriental decoration! Grotefend was the first to explain the use of the mysterious wedges. By 1802 he had, with tolerable certainty, read the three proper names of the kings found on an inscription brought from Persepolis, but apart from these three words his conclusions were generally wrong.

Major (later, General, Sir) Henry Rawlinson, the British Representative at Bagdad, at great peril, succeeded in 1835 in copying the bilingual texts of Darius at Behistun near Kermanshah. By 1839 he had read 200 lines of this inscription. In 1847 Edward Hincks, an Irish clergyman, made a great advance towards discovery when he found that cuneiform was not an alphabetical system of writing, and by 1857 he had fixed the value of 252 combinations of wedges. Other scholars confirmed the findings of both Rawlinson and Hincks.

However, a certain amount of skepticism existed regarding the translations made by these scholars, for in 1857 Mr. Fox-Talbot, who was an early student of cuneiform, suggested that a test should be made by giving Rawlinson, Hincks, Oppert and himself an Assyrian cuneiform historical text which had not been published. These scholars agreed to make a translation of it entirely independently of each other and to submit their results to the Royal Asiatic Society, who were to form a committee to compare the translations. This committee found that the results were in agreement on all essential points, so that thereafter doubts were for the most part dispelled, and it was generally acknowledged that the key to the decipherment of the Babylonian cuneiform writing had been found. There were some scholars, however, who still doubted the solutions given; they were puzzled by the fact that a single sign could have more than one syllabic value. This was partly due to the circumstance that the old picture writing had been copied by wedge writing, so that a five-wedge sign placed similar to four fingers and a thumb meant a "hand," and a set of wedges in a crossed star formation, indicated a "star." At length all doubts vanished, and the translation of cuneiform writing has become a relatively accurate science. Since that time a succession of brilliant and able scholars such as S. H. Langdon, C. J. Gadd, A. Poebel, S. N. Kramer and A. Falkenstein have grappled with the continual problems and difficulties presented by the more and more archaic forms of writing which have been unearthed.[2]

Scribes, Tablets and Literary Form

Some important elements of ancient writing must yet be noticed. What literary methods were in use in early days? What style and form did they adopt for their various documents? How and where did they sign and date their letters and other tablets? Seeing that clay tablets cannot be stitched, as can pieces of parchment or the pages of a book, what means were used to connect tablets together and preserve their proper sequence when more than one tablet was necessary to contain a piece of writing? These problems are rarely referred to in popular books on excavation and the student must turn to technical works, the contents of which are largely printed in

[2]More recently, R. A. Briggs, *The Abu Salabikh Tablets* (1975).

cuneiform, in order to obtain an adequate answer to them.

We first notice that when scribes were employed, they not only wrote the whole of the letter, record, or legal tablet but also took the owner's seal and impressed it on the clay; for these scribes knew best just how much pressure the seal should have on the clay to make it distinct. The seal was usually a cylinder from half an inch to an inch and a half long, but sometimes a precious stone engraved and worn on a ring was used. Each seal was specially inscribed for the owner and often included his name in cuneiform. A reference to the use of the seal is found in Job 38:14, "It is changed as clay under a seal." Judah carried a seal about with him, and Joseph was given Pharaoh's seal ring (Gen. 41:42). At Ur of the Chaldees Sir Leonard Woolley found seals owned by men who lived before the Flood. The use of this seal impression was the equivalent of the modern signature. When the owner's seal had been impressed upon the clay, the tablet, if written by a scribe, had sometimes written on it the name of the owner of the tablet. (I have tablets sealed over 4,000 years ago.)

The matter to be inscribed on clay documents varied greatly. There were *historical* tablets containing narrative concerning clans or nations; *legal* tablets relating to the sale of land, buildings, or loans; *commercial* tablets, detailing in a manner similar to a modern invoice, transactions in farm produce, cattle, or common merchandise; *letters*, both official and private, and tablets containing *genealogical lists*.

Anyone familiar with cuneiform tablets can tell almost at a glance the nature of their contents. Just as in the present day the size and style of paper used (whether foolscap or letter paper, parchment or postcard) generally indicates the nature of their contents, such as a legal document, a private letter, or an official communication, so the size and style of Babylonian tablets are similarly indicative of their contents. There were prisms, cylinders, tablets made barrel-shaped and pillow-shaped; some of the latter as big as quarto paper and others as small as a postage stamp.

Ordinarily, clay tablets were made of sufficient size to contain all the writing matter to be inscribed. But in some instances this was only achieved by using a small stylus, thus enabling a larger number of words to be written on the limited space available. It was not considered satisfactory to make a clay tablet too large. This was for two good reasons; firstly its liability to breakage, and next, from consideration of weight and handiness. Instances of tablets eighteen inches by twelve are rare.[3] As a general rule single tablets sufficed for ordinary documents, such as letters, contracts, invoices, and genealogical lists.

Linking a Series of Tablets

When, however, the lengthy nature of the writing required more than one tablet, it was just as necessary then as it is today (with the pages of letters or books) to adopt means to preserve their proper sequence, especially when a considerable number of tablets were required to complete the series. This was achieved by the use of "titles," "catch-lines," and "numbering." *The title was taken from the first words of the first tablet, these were repeated at the end of each subsequent tablet, followed by the serial number of that tablet*; just as a title is often repeated at the head of each page of a book and

---

[3] D. J. Wiseman, *The Vassal-Treaties of Essarhaddon* (1958), p. 1ff.

each page is numbered. By this method, not only the series to which each tablet belonged, but also the order in which they were to be read, was indicated.

As an additional safeguard it was also the practice to use "catch-lines." This system has not entirely lapsed, but is still frequently adopted in writing or typing modern documents of importance. The present usage is to repeat the first two or three words of a subsequent page at the end of the preceding page. In Babylonian tablets the same method was employed, for the first few words of the subsequent tablet are repeated as "catch-lines" at the end of the previous tablet. It will not surprise the student acquainted with ancient or eastern customs, that many of the literary habits were precisely the reverse of our own. The Hebrews commenced their writing on what to us is the last page of the book and wrote from right to left. Similarly we find that in ancient Iraq, it was the ending and not the beginning of a tablet which contained the vital information as to the name of the writer, date on which written, and description of the composition.

We would suggest that there can now be little doubt that initially much of the book of Genesis would have been written on tablets. We know that they were in use in the days of Moses. Similarly, it is very probable that the Ten Commandments were written on tablets (not "tables") of stone, and in a manner similar to Babylonian tablets in "that the tablets were written on both their sides" (Exod. 32:15). The Hebrew verb "to write" means to "cut in" or "dig," a reference to the early method of writing.

In the following chapter we shall show how, on examining the book of Genesis, we find that some of these ancient literary usages are still embedded in the present English text. Just as the scribes of Nineveh 2,500 years ago, when copying tablets which had been written a thousand years earlier, ended the tablet with a short statement indicating from which library the original text had come, we suggest that the compiler of Genesis has done precisely the same.

V

The Key to the Structure of Genesis

It is the purpose of this chapter to demonstrate that the master key to the method of compilation that underlies the structure of the book of Genesis is to be found in an understanding of the phrase "These are the generations of...." If this phrase is handled consistently, the author believes that it will be found to solve the literary and many other difficulties which the book has so long presented.

All scholars appear to agree that this is the most significant and distinguishing phrase in the book. For example, Dr. S. R. Driver says: "The narrative of Genesis is cast into a framework, or scheme, marked by the recurring formula *These are the generations* (lit., begettings or genealogical histories) *of*....' The entire narrative as we now possess it is accommodated to it" (*Genesis*). Professor H. E. Ryle informs us that the use of the phrase "represents, as it were, successive stages in the progress of the narrative." Commentators of all schools of thought, such as G. J. Spurrell, F. Lenormant, J. Skinner, J. E. Carpenter, C. F. Keil, H. Bullinger, J. P. Lange, and C. H. H. Wright divide the book into sections which begin with the phrase. The formula is used eleven times in Genesis. As to its importance there can be no doubt, for so significant did the Septuagint translators regard it, that they gave the whole book the title "Genesis." This is the Greek equivalent of the Hebrew word translated "generations."

The formula is used in the following places:

2:4 These are the generations of the heavens and the earth.

5:1 This is the book of the generations of Adam.

6:9 These are the generations of Noah.

10:1 These are the generations of the sons of Noah.

11:10 These are the generations of Shem.

11:27 These are the generations of Terah.

25:12 These are the generations of Ishmael.

25:19 These are the generations of Isaac.

36:1 These are the generations of Esau.

36:9 These are the generations of Esau.

37:2 These are the generations of Jacob.

Misunderstandings of Some Scholars

But while scholars of all schools of thought are agreed concerning its importance, they seem to have misunderstood both its use and meaning. The reason for this is quite simple. Many of these sections commence, as is frequent in ancient documents, with a genealogy, or a register asserting close family relationships. This has led them to associate the phrase, "These are the generations of...," with the genealogical list where this follows; hence they have assumed that the phrase is used as a preface or introduction. For instance, S. R. Driver writes, "This phrase is one which belongs properly to a genealogical system; it implies that the person to whose name it is prefixed is of sufficient importance to mark a break in the genealogical series, and that he and his descendants will form the subject of the section which follows, until another name is reached prominent enough to form the commencement of a new section" (*Genesis*). Dr. Driver's assertion is plainly contrary to the facts.[1] For if we examine the evidence regarding the latter part of the statement we find that the most prominent person in Genesis is Abraham. He, more than all those mentioned, would be entitled to be named if this interpretation could claim to be true. Yet it is remarkable that while lesser persons are mentioned, there is no such phrase as "These are the generations of *Abraham*." The first part of the statement is also erroneous, for the phrase does not always belong to a genealogical list, for in some instances no genealogical list follows; in fact, the main history of the person named has been written *before* the phrase and most certainly is not written after it. When we read, "This is the book of the generations of Adam," we learn nothing more about Adam excepting his age at death. The record following, "These are the generations of Isaac," is not so much a history of Isaac as that of Jacob and Esau. Similarly, after "These are the generations of Jacob," we read mainly about Joseph. In fact this peculiarity has puzzled most commentators. It is therefore clear that this phrase is *not* an introduction or a preface to the history of a person, as is so often imagined.

Consequently it is of considerable importance to ascertain the precise meaning of this phrase, "These are the generations of...." The Hebrew word for "generations" in this expression is *tōlēdōt* and not the ordinary Hebrew word *dor* which is translated "generations" 123 times.

---

[1] R. K. Harrison, *Introduction to the Old Testament* (Eerdmann's, 1969), discusses this mistake made by some modern scholars (pp. 545-53) and the thesis of this book as applied to Genesis (p. 64).

Fortunately there can be no reasonable doubt about the meaning of this word *tōlēdōt*. Gesenius, the pioneer Hebrew critical scholar, in his lexicon, explains its meaning as "history, especially family history, since the earliest history among oriental nations is mostly drawn from genealogical registers of families. Then also for the origin of anything, i.e., the story of their origin; Genesis 2:4 'this is the origin of the heavens and the earth,' i.e., the story of their origin."

Most Hebrew scholars translate the word in a similar manner. For instance, F. Buhl (17th German ed.), "genealogical history"; F. Boettcher, "history." H. A. C. Havernick says: "*Toledoth* signifies the history of the origin." J. Furst defines it as "generation, creation, commonly an account, a history of a rise, development of a thing." B. J. Roberts, "This is the history"; M. Kalisch, "beginnings"; H. Ewald, "origins"; Rashi (Solomon ben Isaac of Troyes), "productions"; A. Dillman, "forthbringings"; H. E. Ryle "the chronicles." To this day, the Rabbis who are immersed in biblical Hebrew use the word *tōlēdōt* as the equivalent of the ordinary English word "history." The Hebrew collection of Jewish traditions about the life of Jesus is called *Tōlēdōt Ješu* and this the Jews always translate *History of Jesus*. Even S. R. Driver sees that the word *tōlēdōt* is so used, for in commenting on Genesis 25:19, he writes, "The generations of Isaac (according to the principle followed by the compiler), the *history* of Isaac and his descendants." On Genesis 37:1 he refers to the phrase as "P's introduction to the *history* of Jacob."

The Meaning of Family Histories

It will be seen, therefore, that the word is used to describe *history*, usually family history *in its origin*. The equivalent phrase in English is, "These are the historical origins of... " or "These are the beginnings of...." It is therefore evident that the use of the phrase in Genesis *is to point back to the origins of the family history* and not forward to a later development through a line of descendants. This is made abundantly clear from the only occasion of its use in the New Testament, where in Matthew 1:1, we read, "The book of the generations of Jesus Christ," following which is a list of ancestors. Here it certainly means the exact opposite of descendants, for it is used to indicate the tracing back of the genealogy to its origin. This is precisely the meaning of the Greek word *geneseos* translated "generation." So that when we read "this is the book of the history of Adam" it is the concluding sentence of the record already written and not an introduction to the subsequent record.

The first use of the phrase is in chapter 2:4, "These are the generations of the heavens and the earth." In this one instance we find that scholars have generally placed the formula in its right position, for they have seen that it obviously points back to the narrative of the Creation contained in the previous chapter and that it cannot refer to the narrative that follows, for this section contains no reference to the creation of the heavens. The phrase is only appropriate as a concluding sentence. So most commentators, notwithstanding their usual opposite interpretation of the words, make the story of the Creation *end* with them. Had they seen that *all* sections of Genesis are *concluded* by the use of this formula they would have recognized the key to the composition of the book.

Examples of Misunderstanding

It is because commentators have seen so clearly that "These are the generations (or origins) of the heavens and the earth," in its first use, *ends* that narrative, that they have found themselves in such serious difficulties in their assumption that its use in all the remaining passages is as a commencing phrase. In order to make their interpretation consistent they have endeavored to change the position of the phrase. Thus G. J. Spurrell in his commentary on the Hebrew text of Genesis writes: "In this chapter no history of the heavens and the earth follows; so E. Schrader and others suppose that this half-verse properly ought to precede chapter 1:1, its present position being perhaps due to the compiler of the book who inserted it here in order to form a transition to chapter 2:4bff." And J. E. Carpenter and G. Harford-Battersby (*The Hextateuch*) write of the formula that it "is not appropriate to the narrative that follows it in chapter 2:4b," and say it should be transferred to the beginning of the section. Continuing this remarkable method of reasoning, Dr. J. Moffatt in his translation of the Bible has deliberately altered the text by taking this sentence out of chapter 2:4 and placing it at the beginning of the first chapter of the Bible. These scholars have no manuscript authority whatever for this transposition of the text; but having inherited or assumed an incorrect interpretation of the use of the formula, they think it necessary to do violence to the text by moving it from the end to the beginning of the section, for it is obvious to them (but why in this instance only?) that the words can only refer to what has gone before, that is, to the narrative of the Creation.

Another illustration may be taken from *Ellicott's Commentary*. On Numbers 3:1 ("Now these are the generations of Aaron and Moses"), it says: "the word generations here, as in the book of Genesis and elsewhere, is used to denote the history." Then having lapsed into the usual assumption that it can only refer to the *history* of the descendants, it proceeds on this supposition to give a long and involved explanation in an endeavour to account for the fact that "we find in this place no mention of the sons of Moses." Had the phrase been interpreted correctly it would have been clear that the reference was backward to the record already written (about or by Aaron and Moses) and not forward to the history of their sons.

In two instances only, in Genesis, does a genealogical list follow the sentence without intervening words, and both these lists are quite complete without its use. Also, the formula is not necessarily connected with a genealogical list at all, although in almost every instance a list of immediate descendants is given *before* the phrase as well as after it. "These are the generations of the heavens and the earth" has obviously nothing to do with the list of descendants; neither have the two sentences in 37:2 ("These are the generations of Jacob. Joseph being seventeen years old was feeding the flock with his brethren") any immediate connection with each other. "These are the generations of Jacob" ends one section of history; "Joseph being seventeen years old," etc., commences another section.

Early Babylonian Records

In the early days in Babylonia, the most treasured tablets were those containing the record of ancestors and the appropriate place for such a genealogical list is at the *beginning* of a tablet. That it was quite customary to give a genealogical list at the commencement can be seen from the beginnings of such books as Exodus and Chronicles. When this is understood it clears away the great difficulty out of which commentators have labored to extricate themselves in endeavors to account for the absence of a genealogical list after the formula. An instance of this may be cited from William Paul's *Analysis and Critical Interpretation of the Hebrew Text*. On Genesis 6:9, he says: "This is the record of the history of

Noah, for so 'Toledoth' is rendered by Rosenmuller, Gesenius and Lee here and in Genesis 2:4." He then lapses into the conventional assumption that a genealogical table must necessarily follow, but states: "There is here no genealogical account of Noah's pedigree, with the exception of the mention of his three sons of whom previous notice was taken." It is therefore evident that the formula is not a preamble to a genealogical list but an ending to such a list or narrative. This may be seen from numerous early tablets.

The genuineness of these Genesis records and their uncorrupted state, is surely attested by this adherence to the prevailing literary method of ancient writing, where we find little or nothing by way of preface, but frequently a very formal conclusion. In contradistinction to its simple opening, the conclusion of Leviticus is, "These are the commandments which the Lord commanded Moses for the children of Israel in Mount Sinai," and the last sentence of Numbers reads: "These are the commandments and judgments which the Lord commanded by the hand of Moses unto the children of Israel in the plains of Moab by Jordan near Jericho." One instance outside Scripture may be cited, that of the Code of Hammurabi, the king who was contemporary with Terah and Abraham. Here again the conclusion is more lengthy and formal than the preface. It is at the end of his great inscription that he speaks of having written it. He says, "The righteous laws which Hammurabi the wise king established...my weighty words have I written upon my monument."

Now the Genesis method is the general literary method of early times. But commentators, having assumed that the formula begins a section and not realizing that it *ends* it, have used this key to its compilation upside down, and consequently the problem of the composition of the book of Genesis has remained unsolved by them. For instance, J. Skinner wrote just before he died in 1929: "The problem of the *Toledoth* headings has been keenly discussed in recent writings, and is still unsettled (*Genesis*)."

Other Important Features

Another important fact needs to be emphasized in connection with this formula's use. On its second mention (5:1) we read: "This is the *book* of the origins of Adam." Here the word *seper*, translated "book," means "written narrative," or as F. Delitzsch translates it, "finished writing." Moreover, the Septuagint Version renders chapter 2:4: "This is the *book* of the origins of the heavens and the earth." The "books" of that time were tablets; the word simply means "record." The earliest records of Genesis, therefore, claim to have been written down, and not as is often imagined passed on to Moses by word of mouth. We are, of course, not sure who wrote the original tablet containing Genesis 1. The archaeological and other evidence, however, strongly suggests that anything up to the time that Abraham left Ur of the Chaldees was written on tablets. As we have sought to show in a previous chapter, the Ten Commandments were written on tablets.

Finally, a careful examination of the use of the name of the person stated at the end of "These are the origins of..." makes it clear that it refers to the owner or writer of the tablet, rather than to the history of the person named; that is, "These are the origins of Noah" does not necessarily mean "This is the history *about* Noah," but the history written or possessed by Noah. When in 11:27, we read: "These are the generations of Terah," we do not read much about Terah, for it simply records that he was the son of Nahor. The phrase is intended to indicate that Terah either wrote, or had written for him, the list of his ancestors found in verses 10-27. Nowhere is there "These are the generations of Abraham," yet his story has been fully written, for we are told that Isaac and Ishmael wrote or owned the tablets containing it. In the early days of writing, it was often the practice to impress the name of the scribe at the end of the tablet. The formula "These are the generations of..." may have been inserted by Moses, the compiler. It is possible that the patriarchs mentioned in Genesis did not with their own hands impress the cuneiform or other ancient script on the stone or plastic clay; in some instances a scribe may have been employed.

To summarize, we have noted three things about this phrase:

(1) It is the *concluding sentence* of each section, and therefore points backward to a narrative already recorded.

(2) That the earliest records claim to have been *written.*

(3) It normally refers to the *writer* of the history, or the owner of the tablet containing it.

The book of Genesis, therefore, contains the following series of tablets possessed by the persons whose names are stated. All of these tablets could have come into the possession of Moses, who compiled the book as we now have it, in the way that family records were normally handed down.

Tablet series		*Contents*
1	1:1—2:4	This is the book of the origins of the heavens and the earth.
2	2:5—5:2	This is the book of the origins of Adam.

3	5:3—6:9a	These are the origins (or histories) of Noah.
4	6:9b—10:1	These are the origins (or histories) of the sons of Noah.
5	10:2—11:10a	These are the origins (or histories) of Shem.
6	11:10b—11:27a	These are the origins (or histories) of Terah.
7-8	11:27b—25:19a	These are the origins (or histories) of Ishmael and Isaac.
9-11	25:19b—37:2a	These are the origins (or histories) of Esau and Jacob.

In this way Moses clearly indicates the source of the information available to him and names the persons who originally possessed the tablets from which he gained his knowledge. These are not arbitrarily invented divisions; they are stated by the author to be the framework of the book.

Two Supporting Facts

Two remarkable confirmations of these divisions are:

(1) In no instance is an event recorded which the person or persons named could not have written from his own intimate knowledge, or have obtained absolutely reliable information.

(2) It is most significant that the history recorded in the sections outlined above, ceases in all instances before the death of the person named, yet in most cases it is continued almost up to the date of death or the date on which it is stated that the tablets were written.

In confirmation of the first point, it will be seen in a later chapter that these narratives bear all the marks of having been written by those who were personally acquainted with the events recorded. These valuable personal histories were not entrusted, as is generally supposed, merely to the memory of man to be handed down century after century by word of mouth. Writing was prevalent at a very early date, and of all the things to be put down in writing, few were of more importance than the events recorded in the early chapters of Genesis. Moreover, we know that in the most ancient times men concerned themselves with writing about the very things which have been preserved for us in the earlier part of this book; the stories of Creation and the Flood were among the oldest and most frequently written of the historical tablets. We have tablets from Babylonia written 4,000 years ago relating to the Creation and the Flood. It is true that these Babylonian accounts are grotesque when compared with Genesis, but they were written 600 years before Moses was born, and even at this date were only copies of tablets that had been written centuries before.

The second corroboration is that in almost every instance where it is applicable, the history contained in the section indicated ends just before the death of the person whose name is given at the conclusion of the tablet. Nine persons are mentioned. Tablet 1 bears no name, it simply reads: "These are the origins of the heavens and the earth."

Tablets 2-11

An examination of the remaining sections reveals that in:

Tablet 2 (2:5—5:2), the history ceases abruptly with Tubal-cain, the "instructor of every artificer in brass and iron"; Jabal, "the father of such as dwell in tents and have cattle"; Jubal "the father of all such as handle the harp and organ"; and Tubal-cain "the forger of every cutting instrument of brass and iron." These men were the eighth generation from Adam, and a comparison with the chronology given in Genesis 5 shows that this generation lived immediately before Adam's death.

Tablet 3 (5:3—6:9a) written or owned by Noah. The genealogical list ends with the birth of his three sons. This list is followed by a statement concerning the corruption of humankind, revealing that this was the cause of the Flood, which took place when Noah was an old man. In this instance he could have written the story of the Flood. This is contained in the tablets of the "history of the sons of Noah."

Tablet (series) 4 (6:9b—10:1) written or owned by Noah's sons. They contain the account of the Flood and the death of Noah. How long Ham and Japheth lived after Noah's death we are unaware, but we know that Shem survived him by 150 years, hence there is nothing in this section which the sons of Noah could not have written.

Tablet (series) 5 (10:2—11:10) written or owned by Shem. He writes of the birth and the formation into clans of the fifth generation after him. We know that he outlived the last generation recorded in this tablet, that is, the sons of Joktan.

Tablet 6 (11:10—27) written or owned by Terah. Terah's genealogical list registers the death of his father Nahor, while he himself lived on until his son Abraham was seventy-five years old. Had Terah lived another eleven years he would have been able to record the birth of Ishmael, and if for another twenty-five years it would have been possible for him to add, "and Abraham begat Isaac." But the history contained in this tablet ends immediately before his own death. If the words found at the end of the tablet, "and Terah lived seventy years," refer to the date he wrote it, then according to the Samaritan

Pentateuch it was written just one year after the last chronological event mentioned in it, that is, the death of Nahor.

The series of Tablets 7 and 8 (11:27—25:19) written or owned by the two brothers Ishmael and Isaac. The latest chronological statement (25:1-4) refers to the birth of Abraham's great-grandsons, and of their growth into clans. Ishmael died forty-eight years and Isaac one-hundred five years after Abraham. As Abraham would seem to have married Keturah soon after Sarah's death (which occurred thirty-eight years before Abraham died), this period of thirty-eight years added to the remaining one-hundred five years of Isaac's life, is a most reasonable period to assign for the birth of Abraham's great-grandsons by Keturah. This indicates that the history recorded in these tablets ceases just before the death of Isaac, whose name is given as the last writer, for Isaac survived Ishmael by fifty-seven years and records his death.

The remaining Tablets (series) 9, 10, and 11 (25:20—37:2), were the tablets belonging to, or written by, Esau and Jacob. Jacob is the central figure in the record, and the latest chronological statement in them is that of the death of Isaac. Immediately before the ending formula, "these are the origins of Jacob," we read, "and Jacob dwelt in the land of his father's sojourning, in the land of Canaan." This sentence has seemed so isolated that it has been regarded by many to have little relation to the context, yet, as we shall see in a later chapter, it is evidence of the date when and where the tablets were written. Within a few years Jacob had moved down to Egypt. This sentence indicates where he was living when he closed his record. For although he tells us of the death of Isaac, he says nothing whatever of the sale of Joseph into slavery, which occurred eleven years before Isaac's death. Neither does he tell of Joseph's interpretation of the butler's dream or of any other event in Egypt. Until Jacob went down to Egypt (ten years after he had buried his father), thus leaving "the land of his father's sojourning," he could not know anything whatever about these things. Thus the record of Jacob closes precisely at the period indicated in the sentence in 37:1. He had gone back to the south country, Hebron (where his father lived), only ten years before Isaac had died, and he records his death. Within ten years of this latter event, Jacob was himself living in Egpyt. So this previously obscure verse of Genesis 37 clearly indicates not only that Jacob wrote the tablets but when and where they were written.

It cannot be a mere coincidence that each of these sections or series of tablets should contain only that which the person named at the end of them could have written from personal knowledge. Anyone writing even a century after these patriarchs, could and would never have written thus. It is therefore abundantly clear that this important formula, "These are the origins of...," which is acknowledged by almost every scholar to be the framework on which the records of Genesis are constructed, is *consistently* used by the compiler. It is often a rule in Scripture that the first use of a word or phrase fixes its future meaning, and we have seen that the obvious and admitted meaning it bears in its first use in chapter 2:4, is appropriate in the remaining instances of its use in Genesis. Thus we are delivered from the labyrinth of conflicting guesses and given clearly indicated sources. These are the names of the persons who wrote or owned the tablets from which Moses compiled the book.

VI

The Great Age of the Book

Every part of the book of Genesis furnishes evidence that it was compiled in the present form by Moses and that the documents from which he compiled it were written much earlier. The various lines of evidence may be summarized as follows:

(1) The presence of Babylonian words in the first eleven chapters.

(2) The presence of Egyptian words in the last fourteen chapters.

(3) Reference to towns which had either ceased to exist, or whose original names were already so ancient in the time of Moses, that as compiler of the book, he had to insert the new names, so that they could be identified by the Hebrews living in his day.

(4) The narratives reveal such familiarity with the circumstances and details of the events recorded, as to indicate that they were written by persons concerned with those events.

(5) Evidences that the narratives were originally written on tablets and in an ancient script.

Babylonian and Egyptian Words

The early chapters of Genesis contain Babylonian words; in fact, it is said by some linguistic experts that the whole environment of these chapters is Babylonian. As these chapters claim to have been written down by persons then living in that country, this is what we would expect. It is a strong indication that they were written at a very early date. How do the experts account for the fact that the only definitely Babylonian words are to be found in the earlier chapters of Genesis and not in the latter part of the book or in the rest of the Pentateuch? It is impossible to suggest that they found their way into these particular chapters after the Hebrews' second contact with Babylon in the days of Daniel or Ezra. For even the most critical scholars admit that these accounts had been written before then.

When the narrative reaches the point at which Joseph arrives in Egypt, the whole environment changes. We find definite Egyptian names such as "Potiphar, the captain of the guard" (37:36) or "Zaphnathpaaneah and Asenath" (41:45). A. S. Yahuda's testimony regarding this is weighty. We find ourselves removed from the simple country life of the patriarchs in Palestine and introduced to the customs of a Pharaoh and the constitution of a kingdom. We are told of the particular method by which the land was granted to the Egyptian priests (47:22); that Joseph has a gold chain about his neck and that runners who went before his chariot demand homage to him as to the highest official of the court (41:42). When Joseph's brethren come down to Egypt he does not eat with them, "because the Egyptians might not eat bread with Hebrews, for that is an abomination to the Egyptians"—a statement which I submit would never have been written at a time later than Moses. Finally, we are told how the bodies of Jacob and Joseph were embalmed in accordance with the normal Egyptian custom, and of the forty days that this process occupied. The person who wrote these chapters was intimately acquainted with Egyptian life and thought.

Lost Cities and New Place Names

There is one sentence—probably the most important piece of evidence of all—which must be added to the five lines of evidence already indicated. In Genesis 10:19 we read, "and the border of the Canaanite was from Zidon as thou goest towards Gerar unto Gaza; as thou goest towards *Sodom and Gomorrah*." This sentence arrests attention, for it must have been written before the overthrow of Sodom and Gomorrah, which took place in Abraham's day. So completely were those cities blotted out that all trace of them became lost and it was believed that they were buried beneath the Dead Sea. In our study of the sources we have seen that this sentence occurs in Shem's tablet, and in his day Sodom and Gomorrah were still standing.

The third line of evidence is that many of the original place names given in Genesis were so old, even in the age of Moses, that it became necessary for him to add an explanatory note, in order to identify these ancient names for the sake of the children of Israel entering the land after their exodus from Egypt. Several instances of this may be seen in Genesis 14. When in the time of Abraham this tablet was written, it recorded the movements of certain kings, and the names of the places, as they were *then* known, were put down. But in the 400 years that elapsed between Abraham and Moses, some of these names had become changed, or the localities were unknown to the Israelites. So Moses, with this ancient text (Genesis 14) before him, in compiling the book of Genesis, added a note to enable his readers to identify place names. Thus we have:

Bela (which is Zoar) verses 2 and 8.
Vale of Siddim (which is the Salt Sea) verse 3.
En-mishpat (which is Kadesh) verse 7.
Hobah (which is on the left hand of Damascus)
    verse 15.
Valley of Shaveh (which is the King's Dale)
    verse 17.

These are the only occasions in which these ancient names are used in the Bible.

Further instances of the use of notes to explain ancient names or localities are to be found in 16:14: Beer-la-hai-roi (behold it is between Kadesh and Bered); in 35:19 we read of Ephrath (which is Bethlehem); in 23:2 we are told that "Sarah died in Kirjath-arba (the same is Hebron in the land of Canaan)." This quote is of special interest as it was necessary to give not only its modern name but even to say that Hebron was in the land of Canaan. This surely indicates that the note was added at a very early date and before the children of Israel had entered the land. No one in later times would need to be told where Hebron was. The children of Israel must have known it quite well after its capture in Joshua's day, when the city was given to Caleb for an inheritance. It then became one of the "cities of refuge" and as such must have been familiar throughout the land. Besides all this, David was king in Hebron for seven years. On the other hand, it would be necessary for a people not yet entered into the land to be told, not only the name of the place where the founders of the race had lived but where this place was situated.

We get a similar note in 23:19: "the cave of the field of Machpelah before Mamre (the same is Hebron in the land of Canaan)." Abraham, Isaac, and Jacob had been buried in this cave of Machpelah; consequently it would have been well known to their contemporaries. But it must be remembered that the whole of the nation excepting Joshua and Caleb had died in the time which had elapsed between leaving Sinai and entering into the land of Canaan. I submit that once the children of Israel had settled in the land, there would be no need of a note to explain where the founders of their race, Abraham, Isaac, and Jacob had been buried. I suggest that these explanations were written for those who were about to enter into the land of Canaan. This supports the view that these notes were written by Moses who died on the margin of the land, immediately before the Israelites had entered into it.

Primitive geographical expressions such as the "south country" (20:1 and 24:62) and "the east country" (25:6) are used in the time of Abraham. These ancient designations never reappear as a description of the countries adjoining the south and east of Palestine. After the time of Genesis they have well-known and well-defined names. I submit that they were written down in *early* days, and no writer after Moses would have used such archaic expressions as these.

Another most significant mark of antiquity in Genesis is to be found in the existence of small "city-states" and of a large number of clans. By the time of Solomon these had ceased to be. This is in contrast to the period of Abraham's life, when Babylon and Egypt were dominated by powerful monarchs ruling from their capitals over vast districts.

Familiarity with Local Detail

In a later chapter we shall look at further facts indicating that these records were written soon after the actual incidents. They were written with so great a familiarity with the details of these happenings, that the conclusion is inevitable that the men who were most concerned in these events had written them down soon after their occurrence. An instance of this may be cited in the action of Sarah with her maid Hagar, in relation to the birth of Ishmael. The procedure followed both by Abraham and Sarah was precisely that laid down in the law then in existence as evidenced by laws 144-46 of the Code of Hammurabi. In Mosaic times quite another law was ordained in Deuteronomy. The modern hypothesis that these incidents are a selection made for religious purposes does not agree with the facts. For, as in other parts of Scripture, the narrative recounts the weakness as well as the strength of the patriarchs; their sins as well as their virtues. The records have not been idealized but left in their ancient and truthful reality.

Evidence of Tablets in the Text

The fifth and final series of evidences for the antiquity of Genesis is found in the various indications that these records were originally written on tablets and in accordance with ancient methods. In Babylonia the size of the tablet used depended upon the quantity of writing to be inscribed thereon. If this was sufficiently small, it was written on one tablet of a size that would satisfactorily contain it. When, however, the quantity to be inscribed was of such a length that it became necessary to use more than one tablet it was customary:

(1) To assign to each series of tablets a "title."

(2) To use "catch-lines," so as to ensure that the tablets were read in their proper order (see Chapter 4).

In addition, many tablets ended with a colophon. This was the equivalent of the modern title page. However, on ancient tablets it was placed at the end of the written matter, instead of at the beginning as is now done. This colophon frequently included among other things:

(3) The name of the scribe who wrote the tablet.

(4) The date when it was written.

There are clear indications in Genesis of the use of some of these methods. As these literary aids relate to the tablets as they came into the possession of Moses, it is of course unlikely that we should find them all in the document as completed by him. That the book was compiled at an early date, certainly not later than the age of Moses, is indicated by the presence of these literary aids. It is remarkable confirmation of the purity with which the text has been transmitted to us, that we find them still embedded in this ancient document.

Evidence of these literary aids may be observed in the following significant repetition of words and phrases connected with the beginning or ending of each of the series of tablets, now incorporated in the book of Genesis.

1:1	God created the heavens and the earth.
2:4	Lord God made the heavens and the earth.
2:4	When they were created.
5:2	When they were created.
6:10	Shem, Ham, and Japheth.
10:1	Shem, Ham, and Japheth.
10:32	After the Flood.
11:10	After the Flood.
11:26	Abram, Nahor, and Haran.
11:27	Abram, Nahor, and Haran.
25:12	Abraham's son.
25:19	Abraham's son.
36:1	Who is Edom.
36:8	Who is Edom.
36:9	Father of the Edomites (lit. Father Edom).
36:43	Father of the Edomites (lit. Father Edom).

The very striking repetitions of these phrases exactly where the tablets begin and end, will best be appreciated by those scholars acquainted with the methods of the scribes in Babylonia, for those were the arrangements then in use to link the tablets together. I submit that the repetition of these words and phrases precisely in those verses attached to the colophon, "These are the origins of,..." cannot possibly be a mere coincidence. They have remained buried in the text of Genesis, their significance apparently unnoticed.

Titles and Dating of Tablets

On cuneiform tablets the "title" was taken from the commencing words of the record. In a similar manner the Hebrew called the first five books of the Bible by titles taken from their opening words. Thus they called Genesis $b^e r\bar{e}\check{s}ît$, the Hebrew for "in the beginning"; Exodus was called $w^{e'}elleh$ $\check{s}^e m\bar{o}t$ ("Now these are the words") the words with which the book commences; so Leviticus is called $wayyiqr\bar{a}'$ ("and he called"); Numbers, $b^e midbar$ ("in the wilderness"); Deuteronomy, had-$d^e barim$ ("the words"). To this day these are the titles given to the first five books of Moses in the Hebrew Bible.

This practice was carried out in the ancient Near East in the following manner. When two or more tablets form a series, they were identified together because the first few words of the first tablet were repeated in the colophon (or title page) of the subsequent tablets, somewhat similar to the way in which the name of a chapter is repeated at the head of each page of a modern book. Where pages of a book were not bound together as they are now, the advantage of this would be obvious. By the repetition of such words as we have listed, the whole of the Genesis tablets were connected together.

In addition, some of these tablets show evidence of "dating." After a tablet had been written and the name impressed on it, it was customary in Babylonia to insert the date on which it was written. In the earliest times this was done in a very simple fashion, for it was not until later that tablets were dated with the year of the reigning king. It was the custom to do it in the following way: "The year in which the throne of Nabu was made," "Year Sumu-el the king built the wall of Sippar," "Year of the canal Tutu-hengal" (presumably the year the canal was cut), "Year Samsuiluna made a throne of gold," and "Year in which canal Hammurabi was dug."

The method of dating the Genesis tablets is seen in the following instances. The end of the first tablet (2:4) reads, "in the day that the Lord God made the earth and the heavens." The sense in which the phrase "in the day" is used may be seen from such a passage as verse 17 of the same chapter, where we read, "in the day that thou eatest thereof thou shalt surely die"; and also verse 2, "God rested on the seventh day from all his works which he had made." At the end of the second tablet (5:1) we read: "This is the book of the origins of Adam *in the day that God created man.*" Later tablets are dated by indicating the dwelling-place of the writer at the time that the colophon was written and these dates are immediately connected with the ending phrase, "these are the generations of.... " Instances of this are:

25:11	And Isaac dwelt by Beer-lahai-roi.
36:8	And Esau dwelt in Mount Seir.
37:1	And Jacob dwelt in the land wherein his father sojourned, in the land of Canaan (RV).

This early method of dating is in agreement with the current literary usage of that early age and also with the rest of the text, as we have noted in a previous chapter. For instance, it was precisely at the time he was living in "the land of his father's sojourning" that Jacob's tablets were written.

Accumulative Evidence of Tablets

I suggest that when this ancient method of "dating" tablets is fully appreciated, and the use of "catch-lines" (referred to in Chapter 4) is understood, it will be seen that we have the means of solving such problems as that presented by the wording of Genesis 11:26-27, "and Terah lived seventy years and begat Abram, Nahor and Haran. Now these are the origins of Terah. Terah begat Abram, Nahor and Haran." The first statement in these verses has been a great stumbling-block to chronologists and commentators, for as it reads, it implies that when Terah was seventy years old, all the three sons named were born to him. But Scripture makes it plain that this was not so, as anyone may see by referring to Acts 7:4 and Genesis 12:4, where it is clear that Abram was not born until sixty years later, that is, when Terah was 130 years old. It is mere speculation to attempt to give the birth dates of the other two sons. To what then does the statement "and Terah lived seventy years" refer? I venture to suggest that (in conformity with the prevailing practice of the times) Terah was "dating" his tablet, that is, indicating that it was written when he was seventy years old. This of course implies acceptance of the Samaritan date of the death of Nahor, the father of Terah, which occurred one year before Terah was seventy. The repetition of the names "Abram, Nahor, and Haran," before and after the formula, or *tōlēdōt*, indicates that they are "catch-lines" and conform to the usual practice of repeating the first words of the subsequent tablet after the last line of its preceding tablet.

Moreover, it would not be an uncommon practice when

tablets relating to ancestors came into possession of a descendant that he should add his own tablet giving his own ancestry. This serves to connect him with the persons and events previously recorded. I suggest that this is just what Terah has done. He has simply added a list of his ancestors (Gen. 11:10-27) connecting him with Shem. Again we must emphasize that such genealogical tablets were general and important in his day. Again, we see that the literary methods employed in connecting together these tablets comprising Genesis are precisely those which were in use in the most ancient times. The writing contained on the tablets in the possession of Abraham (Gen. 1:1—11:27) contain about one-fifth of the number of words which were inscribed on the Stele of Hammurabi, itself composed at a time which may well be the era of Abraham (*ca.* 1750 BC). The brevity of the Bible's earliest records is worthy of note. That of the Creation is the most brief, notwithstanding its importance. All the records before the Flood are concise and brief. Then they gradually expand. Writing before the Flood would probably be less extended than it later became in the time of Abraham. In his day writing had already become common, so we find that the story of his life and of his sons is written in much more detail.

The remaining literary aid was the use of the colophon. This was a final paragraph, sometimes long, in other instances only a few words. Among other things, this appendix usually stated the name of the writer or owner of the tablet. The remnants of this ancient usage may still be seen in periodicals and newspapers where the name of the printer and publisher appear as the last lines of the paper. As we have said, the usual colophon in Genesis is, "These are the origins of...."

To recapitulate, we would emphasize that as such ancient literary aids and cuneiform usages are still discernible, they clearly reveal the purity of the text and the care with which it has been handed down to us. It also signifies that in the earliest times these records were written on clay tablets, and that *these tablets, forming the series from Genesis 1:1—37:1, were joined together in the same manner as we have them today*. We would claim that the evidence of the text of Genesis itself is quite incompatible with the hypothesis advanced by modern scholarship, namely, that Genesis was composed or edited at a much later date from sources which were originally unrelated to each other.

VII

Who Wrote
the Original Tablets?

Before examining in greater detail the substance of
these tablets, it is necessary to recall again the facts
brought to light in recent years regarding the literature
of the period under review. It is now certain that writing
was prevalent before the days of Abraham. To those acquainted with the results of excavation in the Near East,
not only is there no difficulty in believing that the patriarchs caused such records to be written, but in view of
the exceptional nature of the revelation of God to them,
it would be surprising if they had not caused the narrative to be set down in writing.

In January, 1902 M. de Morgan found at Persepolis
three broken pieces of black diorite stone which, when
fitted together, measured nearly eight feet in height and
twenty inches across. On it had been written some 8,000
words in cuneiform, arranged in 4,000 narrow lines and
in forty-nine columns. The number of words contained
on this stone is about a quarter of the number in the
book of Genesis. The writing is cut in to the stone with
considerable care, and the laws reveal a most advanced
state of civilization. If the original tablets which Abraham caused to be written, such as Genesis 14, were now

available, scholars would be able to read his cuneiform writing. The originals of other tablets written long before Abraham's day have been translated by Assyriologists. The fact that the tablets were written 5,000 years ago presents no difficulties to the archaeologists. I myself have witnessed the unearthing of several tablets written soon after the Flood. Of one tablet Professor S. H. Langdon claimed that it was certainly written *before* the Flood. No longer is there any good reason to doubt that the very earliest records in Genesis—those of the Creation and the Fall—were written down in a very early form of writing, within the period that Genesis assigns to Adam's sons.

The First Series of Tablets

Of course, no man could have written the first series of tablets (1:1—2:4) from personal knowledge of the manner in which the world was created. Significantly enough it is the only tablet which does not state the name of the author or writer. It simply says, "These are the generations of the heaven and of the earth." The facts contained in the narrative preserved on this tablet were also beyond the normal outlook of the time. From where did it come? Who wrote it? The second question is not so important as the first. For if it is not a concise account revealed by God of the order of Creation, it is merely a piece of literary speculation. We must face the fact that it contains facts that centuries of modern scientific research, aided by the use of recently perfected instruments of marvelous precision and power, have only lately discovered. Yet so profoundly accurate is this narrative that one scholar (Professor G. W. Wade in his *Old Testament History*) writes of the inherent improbability of an ancient writing anticipating accurately the conclusions of modern science.

Naturally the wording is simple, but the truth conveyed is profound. Human as the language is, it is still the best medium God could use to communicate with man. It is God teaching Adam, in a simple yet faultless way, how the earth and the things which he could see on and around it had been created. The Lord God talked with Adam in the Garden. This tablet purports to be a simple record of what God said and did. Adam is told just as much as his mind could understand. The details and processes are not fully revealed. Had they been, how could he and later ages have understood them? We would claim, then, that this first section of Genesis is the most ancient piece of writing. It is a record of what God told Adam. It is not an *impersonal* general account. It is God teaching the first man the elemental things about the universe, at the very dawn of human language. Here we get back also the very inauguration of written history. For it may have been written before even the sun and moon had been given names. Let us note the simplicity with which the facts are presented. There is a type of repetition and simplicity rarely recurring in Scripture: "Let there be *lights* in the firmament...and God made two *great lights*, the *greater light* to rule the day and the *lesser light* to rule the night."

We know that long before the time of the Flood men worshipped the sun and the moon and had given them names. Had this first chapter of Genesis been written even as late as Abraham's day, instead of the simple expression "greater light" we should have had the Babylonian word for the sun, *šamaš*. It is used in the legal tablet (containing the names of thirteen witnesses) in my personal possession. Moreover, *šamaš* was the name of the sun god worshipped by the Babylonians. In his laws, Hammurabi depicts himself in the attitude of receiving his laws from this *šamaš*. When Abraham left Ur, the moon god was the chief object or worship in that city. The great tower built in the center of the city (at least 250 years before the time of Abraham) was surmounted by a temple dedicated to this moon god. Names for the sun and moon have been among the oldest words known in any language, yet this document was written before names had been given to the "greater and lesser lights."

Features of the First Document

This earliest of all documents is written in a most exceptional way. It is recording the words of God used in telling Adam the story of Creation. Observe the method employed in writing this narrative. "And God said....And God *called*" What God called the components of the universe is placed on record. "And God called the light *day* and the darkness called He *night*....And God called the firmament *heaven*: and God called the dry land *earth* and the gathering together of waters called He *seas*." It is written in the style of someone recording precisely what Adam heard when the narrative was told to him.

Further it is written on a very personal note. It is far removed from the style of a vision. There is no "I saw," "I beheld," "I heard." It is direct speech, "And God said, Behold I have given you every herb yielding seed which is upon the face of all the earth, and every tree in which is the fruit of a tree yielding seed which is upon the face of all the earth, and every tree in which is the fruit of a tree yielding seed to you, and it shall be for meat." These words were spoken to the first man. It is not a vague and general account. All the reader needs to do is to realize its unique features and to compare it with the Babylonian versions.

The Greek (Septuagint) version of the Old Testament

translates the final sentence of this account, "This is the *Book* of the origin of the heavens and the earth." How it came to be written we are not told, but we are informed that language originated in Eden. Adam, who gave names to the living creatures, could conceivably write this short account in the first form of writing. The ancient literary methods, already referred to, show that the tablet could have been in existence by the time of Noah. The use by the Septuagint of the word "Book" indicates that the original account was written down early, though it may have been repeated verbally at first.

This first chapter is so ancient that it does not contain mythical or legendary matter; these elements are entirely absent. It bears the markings of having been written before myth and legend had time to grow, and not as is often stated, at a later date when it had to be stripped of the mythical and legendary elements inherent in every other account of Creation extant. This account is so original that it does not bear a trace of any system of philosophy. Yet it is so profound that it is capable of correcting philosophical systems. It is so ancient that it contains nothing that is merely nationalistic; neither Babylonian, Egyptian, nor Jewish modes of thought find a place in it, for it was written before clans, nations, or philosophies originated. Surely, we must regard it as the original, of which the other extant accounts are merely corrupted copies. Others incorporate their national philosophies in crude polytheistic and mythological form. This is pure. Genesis 1 is as primitive as the first human. It is the threshold of written history.

The Second Series

The second tablet or series of tablets extends from 2:5—5:2 and contains an account of the beginning of man upon the earth, the Garden of Eden, the Fall, and the murder of Abel. This tablet also bears the clearest marks of extreme antiquity and simplicity, which could never have come from a late hand. For instance, the test of obedience is the eating or refraining from eating the fruit of a tree. The tempter is referred to after the Fall as "a serpent in the dust," a form never afterwards used in the Old Testament. Again, it is one that no late writer was likely to employ. Then there are expressions such as "sin crouching at the door" in connection with the story of the offering made by Cain. Also there is the remark of Lamech, "I have slain a young man to my wounding and a young man to my hurt," pointing to contemporary archaic events of which no explanation is given. Again the record shows evidence of being a personal one, "I heard Thy voice in the garden and I was afraid...I hid myself." I suggest that no late writer would have used such intimate phrases as "the Lord God walking in the Garden in the cool of the day." The Jew had been taught a most reverential conception of God, as One infinitely eternal and supreme, the Maker of the heavens and the earth. Even unto Moses God did not appear except in majesty and awe. The expression "cool of the day" is most natural in the Near East; for the greater part of the year it experiences intense heat throughout midday, while in the evening a cool wind blows. Often in Iraq I have heard that expression used to indicate the time immediately after the sun has gone down and the evening wind begins to blow.

The one person who knew all the facts about the Fall is stated to be the source from which the account came. This second tablet takes the story up to the birth of the sons of Lamech. Soon after this Adam died; the concluding words of the tablet are, "This is the book of the origins of Adam."

Noah's Tablet

Noah's tablet comprises 5:3—6:9 and commences with a genealogical register of the patriarchs connecting him with Adam. This list is followed by a statement concerning the corruption extant in his day, together with an explanation of the cause of it. "These are the origins of Noah." It is a small tablet of narrative writing added to a genealogical list.

The Fourth Series

The next series of tablets form 6:9—10:1. We are still in an ancient realm of thought. It commences in a Babylonian scene but ends outside that country. Although for the first time we have moved beyond the confines of the ancient Mesopotamian plain, the writer does not take us to Palestine but to Ararat. We also have the use of that exceptional word "gopher" wood in connection with the construction of the ark. This is most archaic, and the word is never used again. The tablets end with the statement: "These are the origins (or family histories) of the sons of Noah." They are almost wholly taken up with the account of the Flood. This story has received considerable attention from modern scholars who assert that it was borrowed from Babylonia. They have made much of "two accounts" or "three accounts" interwoven into the narrative. J. Astruc, when he came to analyze this story, insisted that it contained three accounts. He instanced such passages as these in Genesis 7:

Verse 18 And the waters prevailed, and were increased greatly upon the earth.

19 And the waters prevailed exceedingly upon the earth.

20 Fifteen cubits upward did the waters prevail.

Also,

Verse 21 And all flesh died that moved upon the face
of the earth.
22 All in whose nostrils was the breath of life
and all that was in the dry land died.
23 And every living substance was destroyed.

It is sufficient here to note two most significant facts.
First, the conclusion of the tablet informs us that more
than one person is connected with the writing of the narrative, for it is the history of the three *sons* of Noah.
Next, that an examination of it reveals every indication
that it was written by several eye-witnesses of the trag-
edy.

The Fifth Series

The fifth series of tablets is contained in 10:2—11:9
and therefore includes the famous tenth chapter—the account of the origins of the clans which became nations.
Embedded in this chapter is a brief statement regarding
Nimrod. In the earlier verses of the eleventh chapter we
have an account of the building of the Tower of Babel
and the scattering of the peoples. Of these records it is
written, "These are the histories of Shem." We have already referred to the significance of the seemingly
abrupt ending of his genealogical list with the "sons of
Joktan," and the repetition and its completion in Terah's
tablet. This tablet of Shems is an outline of developments during the 500 years after the Flood.

The Sixth Series

In 11:10-27 we have the genealogical register belonging to Terah. It gives a list of his ancestors connecting

—93—

him with Shem, the son of Noah. Several such genealogical lists from Babylon are in existence, written long before Terah's.

The Seventh and Eighth Series

The next and longest division (11:27—25:12) is followed by a postscript of seven verses (13-19). In accordance with his usual custom Moses has placed the name of Abraham's eldest son Ishmael (verse 12) before that of Isaac the heir (verse 19). A similar arrangement in the next section places Esau before Jacob; in both instances they were brothers. (It will be noticed in Numbers 3:1 that in a similar way he places Aaron, his elder brother, before himself.) This whole section contains records belonging both to Isaac and Ishmael. It commences with "Terah begat Abraham," and ends with, "and his sons Isaac and Ishmael buried him in the cave of Machpelah."

The intervening chapters are a narrative of all we know of the life of Abraham, the central figure of the book of Genesis. Abraham alone could have recounted most of the incidents, but it would appear that his sons wrote them down, or at least, the copies which we believe that Moses had before him belonged to them. The whole story shows a great familiarity with details. For instance, the visit of the three men recorded in the eighteenth chapter:

> As he sat in the tent door *in the heat of the day*, and he lift up his eyes and looked, and lo, three men stood over against him; and when he saw them he ran to meet them from the tent door, and bowed himself to the earth and said....And he hastened into the tent unto Sarah, and said, Make ready quickly three measures of fine meal....And Abraham ran to the herd and fetched a calf tender and good, and gave it unto his servant and he hastened to dress it...and set it before them; *and he stood by them under the trees*, and they did eat.

The remainder is an intimate personal account of Abraham's prayer for Sodom. After its overthrow we read, *"And Abraham got up early in the morning to the place where he had stood before the Lord*, and he looked toward Sodom and Gomorrah and toward the land of the plain, and beheld and lo, the smoke of the country went up as the smoke of a furnace"* (19:27-28). The style is just what we would expect of Abraham relating the incidents to Isaac who is stated to have owned the tablets containing these events.

The Ninth to the Eleventh Series

The following section (25:19—36:1) is followed by two postscripts contained in chapter 36 concerning Esau in Canaan and Seir. This section (including the postscripts) is, I suggest, the record left by Jacob and Esau. The greater part of the story concerns Jacob, and more than half of it refers to his journey to and from Padan-aram and his life there. He alone could have recorded the events occurring during this period of his life.

It is necessary to bear in mind the place occupied by the patriarchs in the affairs of the time. For instance, Abraham comes into contact with Pharaoh and the princes when he goes into Egypt. In his day Egypt was a mighty power, and he must have had a status that made him a person of prominence in that country, for it was not merely an oriental mode of speech that made the sons of Heth say, "Hear us, my lord: thou art a mighty prince amongst us." We are told that he had "menservants and maidservants," and that "Abram was very rich in cattle, in silver and in gold," and that "their substance was great." So great a person was he, that when he returned to Canaan, he could say to Lot, notwithstanding the presence of the Canaanites in the land, "Let there be no strife, I pray thee, between my herdsmen and thy herdsmen, for we are brethren. *Is not the whole land before thee*? Separate thyself, I pray thee, from me: if thou wilt take the left hand, then I will go to the right, or if thou take the right hand then I will go to the left....And Lot chose him the plain of Jordan, and Abraham dwelt in Canaan" (13:8-12).

In such a manner the choice was made where he would live, and thus the scene is set for the next chapter where he meets the four kings, among them one so mighty as Amraphel, King of Shinar. When these four kings from the East easily overcame the five petty city-state kings of Transjordan, we read that,

> When Abraham heard that his brother Lot had been taken captive, he led forth his trained men born in his own house, three hundred and eighteen, and pursued them as far as Dan....And smote them and brought back all the goods, and also brought again his brother Lot, and his goods, and the women also, and the people....And Abraham said unto the King of Sodom, I have lift up my hand unto the Lord God Most High, possessor of heaven and earth, that I will not take a thread nor a shoelatchet nor aught that is thine, lest thou should say I have made Abraham rich.

In a like manner Isaac and Jacob are depicted as possessing considerable status in their day, and they are quite capable of writing or employing scribes to write the tablets containing narratives from which Moses compiled the account.

The Rest of the Book

But who wrote the last fourteen chapters of Genesis? It is mainly a history of Joseph in Egypt, at least the family history centers around him. This record begins with the words, "and Joseph being seventeen years old," and ends with "and he (Joseph) was put in a coffin in

The excavated ruins in the ancient capital city of Babylon. Scribes, trained here from the third millennium onward, adopted the practice of adding colophons to their literary compositions.

The foundations of the Ishtar gateway at Babylon.

Fragment from the *Epic of Gilgamesh* found at Megiddo, Israel; dated fourteenth century BC. This epic includes one Babylonian account of the Flood.

Fragment of an inscribed clay tablet showing the colophon at the end of a typical Assyrian library tablet. Details given include the text title, date, scribe's name, and the purpose and placement of the text. Found at Ninevah; dated *ca.* 640 BC (British Museum 80-7-19, 277).

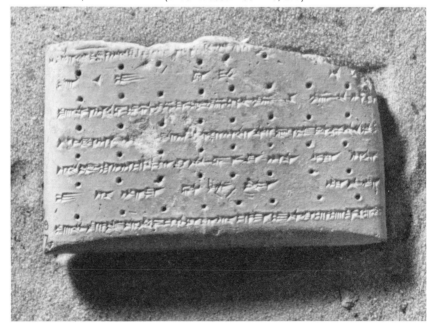

Colophon (left) on reverse
of clay tablet inscribed with the
Atrahasis Epic from Babylon
dated *ca.* 1635 BC but copied
from earlier texts. It records the
creation of humankind, human
rebellion against the gods, and
the sending of the Flood. (British
Museum 78941).

A Sumerian clay prism naming the ten
kings who lived before the Flood. Found
at Kish; dated *ca.* 2000 BC (Ashmolean
Museum, Oxford; WB 444).

Reverse of a baked clay tablet inscribed with hemerological omens. The colophon indicated that this was a copy of a standard text, known earlier from Ur and Babylon, made by the high-priest of King Ashurnasirpal II at Nimrud (biblical Calah) ca. 870 BC. The lug at the foot was for mounting the text on a swivel for ease of turning as a reference work. (Nimrud, ND 5545).

Egypt." This section, as we have seen, contains many purely Egyptian words and phrases, as well as intimate references to Egyptian modes of life. In this section we have passed from Babylonia to Egypt where in all probability it would be written on papyrus. Unlike other sections it has no ending formula to indicate who the author is. This question forms part of the problem considered in the following chapter.

VIII

Was Moses the Compiler?

What we have suggested as the explanation of the narratives and genealogies of which Genesis 1-36 is composed, having been advanced on the basis stated in Genesis itself, it remains to consider the work of Moses in relation to the completed book.

On examining it we discover that the name of Moses is not mentioned. Nowhere in Scripture is there a statement that Moses actually wrote the narratives or genealogies of Genesis. In Genesis we have no statements referring to Moses in the same way as, or similar to, those so often repeated in Exodus, Leviticus, Numbers, and Deuteronomy: "The Lord said unto Moses" or "God spake unto Moses saying." Surely this is a most remarkable and significant fact. Modern critical scholars have told us repeatedly that we can ignore such phrases as claims to authorship. They suggest that they were used inaptly, and lavishly inserted by later writers or editors, who wished the readers to believe that what they themselves had written had actually been spoken to Moses directly by God. It was done, so we are told, in order to claim for their writings the great authority of Moses.

If this is so, how do these scholars account for the complete absence from Genesis of any reference to Moses?—especially as they assert that these alleged writers and editors most certainly included Genesis in the writings which they wished to attribute to Moses, and for which they desired to claim the cover of his traditional authority. Surely the fact that the phrase, "The Lord spake unto Moses, saying," does not appear in Genesis, counts strongly against such editors and redactors. For they appear not to have touched the original text of Genesis. Furthermore, the non-occurrence of this phrase in the book is surely a clear indication that, when it is used in the remaining "Books of Moses," it is likely to have been used authentically and accurately, and that there also the text has been preserved in a pure state.

The New Testament method of referring to the Books of Moses is also worthy of note. It is a significant example of the accuracy with which references to authorship are made in the Bible. Although Christ and the apostles repeatedly quote from Genesis, they never actually say that Moses wrote or spoke the statement quoted. When, however, we read references or quotations taken from the beginning of Exodus and onwards to Deuteronomy, it is then we begin to read in the New Testament, "Moses said."

Evidence of Moses

What internal evidence, then, have we of any connection of Moses with the book? In the first place, there is the obvious unity of plan that it presents. Secondly, there is the authorship of the story of Joseph in Egypt. Moses was learned in all the arts of the Egyptians; his acquaintance with the literature of Egypt and ability to write the language was perhaps his greatest asset. He was born sixty-four years after Joseph had died. Joseph may have written a great part of his story, but we are not told that he did so, for there is no such phrase as, "These are the origins of Joseph," at the end of Genesis. Besides, in this instance Joseph's death and embalming are recorded, and he could not have written that. The whole of the story contains numerous Egyptian expressions and shows an exact acquaintance with Egyptian customs. Every indication points to Moses as the writer of the narrative. Thirdly, there are the "notes" and "explanations" made by the compiler. These (as we have seen in Chapter 6) fit in exactly with the circumstances of a people on the edge of the Promised Land, for whom Moses was writing. The fourth piece of evidence is that the book of Exodus commences just where Genesis leaves off. Exodus is unintelligible without the explanation, given in Genesis, of the circumstances leading up to the state of affairs with which it opens.

It is worthy of comment that though many learned works have been written to defend the Mosaic authorship of the Pentateuch, these say next to nothing about the direct connection of Moses with the greater part of Genesis. For instance, so able and accurate a writer as the late Dr. W. H. Green of Princeton, in his valuable volumes on this subject, gives many excellent reasons why Moses wrote the laws contained in Exodus to Deuteronomy, but he leaves Genesis isolated. Dr. Adam Young writes of Moses that, "his authorship of Exodus, Leviticus, Numbers and Deuteronomy, is attested by every possible mark of an internal and of an external kind," but no mention is made of Genesis. Others speak of "four-fifths of the Pentateuch claiming to have come from Moses." The first fifth, Genesis, has been neglected.

Sources of Information

It would seem that conservative scholars, though accepting the Mosaic composition of Genesis, have not found it practicable to indicate exactly the manner in which he received his information. Doubtless the reason why most have hesitated to say that he received the whole as we have it, as a direct revelation from God on Mount Sinai, is a very sufficient one: he himself does not say that he did so. Surely, had he so received it, Moses would have stated the fact, just as he so constantly does from Exodus to Deuteronomy. There is a distinction between a direct revelation of the original narratives or genealogies from God and the full inspiration afforded Moses by God in its compilation. The end achieved by God is the same. Luke wrote in his gospel record by "having traced the course of all things accurately from the first," but the divine inspiration of Luke's gospel was none the less because of this. There have been many eminent scholars who have suggested, and some who have asserted, that Moses used previously written documents from which he compiled Genesis. None, however, so far as I am aware, have even suggested the precise nature of the documents that came into his possession, notwithstanding the fact that such information is given in Genesis.

There would seem to be three reasons for this. Firstly, it is due, as we have seen in Chapter 5, to a misunderstanding of the use of the phrase, "These are the generations (or origins) of...," and secondly, to a lack of acquaintance with, or oversight of, the literary methods prevalent in the times of Genesis. These methods, such as dating, catch-lines, titles, and colophons, are rarely referred to except in technical archaeological works. Thirdly, it is due to acquiescence in the now obsolete but commonly accepted opinion that the contents of Genesis were handed down to Moses by word of mouth. The long ages to which the pre-Flood patriarchs lived is emphasized to show that oral transmission would have needed to pass through but few memories. There is, however, nothing whatever in Genesis, or elsewhere, that asserts an oral transmission. It was, perhaps, not possible until the results of more recent excavations had become known, to read such a verse as 5:1, "This is the book (tablets) of...," as though it could mean precisely what it says. This oral transmission theory originated at a time when men were unacquainted with the facts concerning the early development of writing.

The early origin of writing needs to be emphasized again. It is scarcely possible to put too strongly the importance of the fact that the archaeological museums of the world now possess thousands of tablets from the ancient Near East. Hundreds of them were written before Abraham's day and many before the birth of Moses. Included amongst them are accounts of the Creation and the Flood. We can now at least give Genesis credit for speaking the truth and for stating precisely what it intends to convey when it refers to such records. Moses did not use a collection of stories which had descended to him by word of mouth, for he himself informs us, at the end of the various narratives and genealogies, who had written or owned them. These, commencing at the dawn of history, had accumulated as Noah, Noah's sons, Terah, Isaac, and Jacob.

Transmission of Tablets

How did these tablets get into the hands of Moses? They contained records from the creation of Adam to Moses' own time. We suggest that the internal evidence of the book indicates the tablets of Creation were extant in the time of Noah, and we suggest that the record of the Garden and the Fall (to which Moses added a geographical description) had been written by this time. These would descend to Noah, for we notice that in his own tablet (5:29) he makes a reference (3:17) to the first tablet. Noah added the genealogical list contained in chapter 5. Already several cuneiform tablets bearing some resemblance to this chapter have been found; they refer to ten men who "ruled before the Flood." Noah's tablet is simple and straightforward compared with these, and the ages given are not a tenth of those stated in the Babylonian tablets. Noah also adds a short statement regarding the corruption existing in the world in his day. His sons, we are informed in Genesis, wrote the account of the Flood, while Shem wrote the genealogical list which now occupies chapter 10, as well as the brief description of the building of the Tower of Babel. Thus we see how Noah, possessing the tablets relating to the Flood, these including his own (Genesis 10 and the Tower of Babel), would naturally pass down to Abraham, with the genealogical tablet written by his father Terah. Thus to him were committed these ancient "oracles of God" (that is Genesis 1—11:27.)

This does not by any means imply that copies were not made by other members of these families. There is every reason to believe that they were made. A scrutiny of the later copies of these copies, which excavators have dug up, however, reveal that they had become hopelessly corrupted very early by the introduction of dozens of contemporary gods into the Creation tablets, and a similar distortion befell the Flood tablets. On the other hand, all scholars would recognize that the records preserved for us in Genesis are pure and free from all these corruptions which penetrated into the Babylonian copies.

The archaeological evidence suggesting that the second series of tablets relating the story of the Fall was joined to the first recording of the story of Creation was presented in Chapter 6. We have also seen the way that the sons of Noah joined their accounts of the Flood to their copy of Noah's tablet by a repetition of certain words, and the manner in which Shem connected his tablet with the previous tablets of which he appears to have had copies.

We would claim that the archaeological evidence suggests that a tablet such as Terah's was written in the ordinary cuneiform script used at Ur of the Chaldees. But the earlier tablets were probably written in a more ancient script, and these would possibly be transcribed into the current language of the day. Abraham, coming into possession of these precious documents telling of the God of his fathers (the one God, the Creator of the heavens and the earth), was called by God to leave Ur for Canaan. The most sacred possession that he would carry with him were these tablets. Some uncertainty still exists about the language spoken in Palestine at the time of Abraham's arrival there,[1] though we know that 600 years later correspondence with both Babylonia and Egypt was still conducted in cuneiform script. This was the script of the educated. There can be little doubt that Isaac and Jacob would have used this script when writing their tablets.

When Jacob moved with all he had down to Egypt, he would carry with him the narratives and genealogies of the book of Genesis up to 37:1, for Jacob tells us that he had written his own account while "he lived in the land of his father's sojourning, in the land of Canaan." As we have noticed in Chapter 6, we possess ancient evidence that Isaac's tablet was joined with Terah's by the use of a "catch-line," and that the remainder of the tablets, Esau's and Ishmael's, were also connected with Jacob's in the manner prevalent in that day. So, in Jacob's time

---

[1] This may well be ellucidated by the find of about 16,000 tablets at Ebla (Tell Mardih in Syria) in 1975-77, dated *ca.* 2300 BC.

these tablets comprising Genesis 1-36 were connected together as one record.

Joseph to Moses in Egypt

In Egypt they became the heritage of Joseph and the family then developing into a nation. They would naturally pass into the hands of Moses, not necessarily the actual originals (though stone and baked clay are the most imperishable forms of writing material known) but true copies of these originals. An educated Egyptian of his day would be able to read cuneiform writing with as much facility as a classical scholar today is able to read Greek or Latin. At the time of Moses this cuneiform writing was the current diplomatic script, and the dispatches received at the Egyptian Foreign Office, from eastern lands, were in this script. The hundreds of Tel-el-Amarna tablets are examples of such correspondence. Moses, learned in the arts of the Egyptians, would readily be able to read and, if necessary, to translate them.

Until Moses was eighty years old these tablets of Genesis were his only Bible. This would appear to be the only way God instructed him, for there is no mention of God speaking directly with him until the end of the forty years in Midian, when he called him to return to Egypt to bring his people into the Promised Land. Then God announced himself by saying: "I am the God of thy father, the God of Abraham, the God of Isaac, and the God of Jacob. And Moses hid his face." God was speaking to him, just as the patriarchs had recorded that he had spoken to them. His mind would be saturated by the Genesis records and with the knowledge of all that this involved.

Although his Bible consisted only of the tablets now contained in the first thirty-six chapters of Genesis, his mind would not be a blank regarding sacred institutions, nor was he dependent on oral traditions as to what God had ordained for the patriarchs. In the second tablet he would read of Abel "bringing the firstlings of his flock, and Cain the fruit of the ground, for an offering unto the Lord," and in Isaac's tablet of that incident in life when the ram was substituted for Isaac on Mount Moriah. The fourth series of tablets would tell him of the "altar which Noah builded," and later tablets how Abraham set up altars at the dwelling places; of giving one-tenth to Melchizedek, and of Jacob vowing a tenth to God. The centuries before Moses were not dark ages unilluminated by God. God had not left his people without a written revelation. At various times and in different forms he had spoken to Adam, Noah, Abraham, Isaac, and Jacob, and their records had been written on tablets, in the manner customary at that time. The revelation of God in Genesis, as it was handed down to Moses had not been dependent on the memory of man during the centuries which had elapsed.

The Scribe for God

Moses became the leader of the nation, and we are informed that as soon as he left Egypt he began his career as a scribe for God. It is possible that he used the tablets, for the Ten Commandments were probably written on two tablets (not tables) of stone, and written in the usual manner on both sides. As we have noted, the Hebrew verb "to write" means "to cut in," a possible reference to the original method of writing on tablets. When the Israelites had crossed over into Sinai, and immediately after their battle with Amalek, we read: "And the Lord said unto Moses, Write this for a memorial in a book" (Exod. 17:14). After God had given the covenant to him on Mount Sinai, we read: "And the Lord said unto Moses: Write thou these words,...and he wrote *upon the tablets* the words of the covenant" (Exod. 24:4). Of the stages of their journeyings we are told: "And Moses wrote their goings out according to their journeys by the command of the Lord" (Numb. 33:2).

The endings of the books of Leviticus and Numbers, where we are told that they were written by the hand of Moses, are further illustrations of this. Also in Deuteronomy 27:2-3 we read: "And it shall be on the day when ye shall pass over Jordan into the land which the Lord thy God giveth thee, that thou shalt set thee up great stones, and plaister them with plaister, and thou shalt write upon them all the words of this law." In verse 8 they are told to write this "very plainly"; then in 31:9, "And Moses wrote this law, and delivered it unto the priests." In the same chapter there is a very interesting account of how Moses "the same day" wrote the words of a song: "Now therefore write ye this song for you, and teach it the children of Israel....So Moses wrote the song the same day." The reason for having this written at once is stated in verse 21, "for it shall not be forgotten out of the mouths of their seed, for I know their imagination...even now." In this same chapter we read: "And it came to pass, when Moses had made an end of writing the words of this law in a book until they were finished." This writing on that day ended the forty years of Moses' literary career.

It would seem certain from the "notes" and "explanations" that Moses has given us in Genesis, that they were written by him when he was at the edge of the Promised Land. With these inspired tablets before him, tablets written from the earliest days, he is compiling his book, possibly necessitating the transcription of these ancient records into the current language of the people. Most reverently does he handle them, for they are the record of God's dealing with their fathers of old.

The first thing that impresses us as we read them now, is that he regards the old wording as so sacred that usually he avoids making unnecessary alterations to the text even to modernize words. He leaves the original ancient expressions and place names just as he finds them, though they are no longer in current use. In order that they may be understood by this people—a new generation just entering the land—he explains the ancient records by adding the contemporary place names alongside the ancient names, and sometimes he states that the name is retained "to this day." These "notes and explanations," some of which have been noticed in Chapter 6, are sufficient to interpret ancient usages, to explain or indicate the location of Eden, and to identify patriarchal place names. An examination of such a verse as Genesis 23:17, "And the field of Ephron, which was in Machpelah, which was before Mamre, the field, and the cave which was therein, and all the trees in the field, that were in all the borders round about, were made sure," leaves the impression on the mind of a verbatim extract of the precise wording on a legal tablet such as was used in the days of Abraham. Furthermore, in the Flood tablets, more criticized than any other part of Genesis on account of the "phraseology and style," there are clear indications that the wording has been repeated verbatim from the tablets of the "sons of Noah."

Signs of Reverence for Text

It is evident that Moses held these tablets in such high esteem that he made no attempt whatever to avoid the repetitions or combine the genealogies. Thus, for instance, the genealogies of Shem are found in both 10:22-29 and 11:10-18; also the reference to the corrupt state of the earth and the declaration regarding its destruction, as found in 6:5-8 and 9:13, are left duplicated. We have already seen that these repeated facts belong to tablets written by different patriarchs. Indeed, these repetitions are characteristic of the whole book and are commented upon by almost every reader. It is most significant that with the exception of the section relating the story of the life of Joseph in Egypt, every tablet or series of tablets begins with a repetition of facts contained in the previous tablet. This is precisely what anyone acquainted with the ancient methods of writing would expect and is further evidence of the faithfulness with which the records have been transmitted to us.

It would be to venture off the safe ground of fact, onto the shifting sands of speculation, to go beyond that which is written and attempt to indicate what we are not told. The precise method Moses employed to adapt, connect, and transcribe these tablets, may be a fascinating pursuit, but it would be mere speculation. The facts regarding the origin of the narratives, however, are plainly stated in Genesis, and these need no support from imagination. It is sufficient that all the evidence we have before us indicates that these records have been kept in their original purity when brought together by Moses. The more rigid the test applied to Genesis, the more minute the examination of its contents in general and the words in particular, the more it is read in the light of the newer facts of archaeology, the more irresistibly does it lead us to the conclusion that Moses—the one outstanding man who is named by the consensus of ancient thought and confirmed by all the implication of Scripture—compiled the book, using the pre-existing records, which the patriarchs had named, or he has named, at the end of each section of family histories.

IX

Theories Now Obsolete

If the foregoing approach to the book of Genesis, based upon the findings of ancient Near Eastern archaeological excavations, is correct, then it is clear that many of the earlier theories concerning the compilation and authorship of Genesis were misconceived and are now obsolete. What is known as the higher criticism (theories concerning authorship and composition, as distinct from lower criticism which is concerned with the validity, integrity, and exegesis of the text) has placed the date of Genesis hundreds of years too late.

It is also safe to say that some higher-critical theories would never have seen the light of day, had it not been that they originated in an age unenlightened by archaeological discovery. The fundamental mistakes they made were primarily due to the lack of knowledge concerning ancient times that existed a century ago when these views arose. Their basic misconceptions may be summarized as follows:

(1) Some theories were born in an age of ignorance regarding early civilizations.

(2) The critics attempted a literary analysis when they knew nothing of the early methods of writing.

(3) The majority assumed that writing was not in use in the days of the patriarchs.

(4) Their speculations became dominated by the "myth and legend theory" now generally abandoned.

The First Reason

The first reason why some critical theories are now obsolete is that they were advanced when their proponents were completely ignorant regarding the civilizations of the times of Genesis. Excavations in the Euphrates valley did not begin until the middle of the last century, yet notwithstanding the lack of knowledge which then prevailed, too many scholars thought themselves capable of determining what they imagined to be the literary conditions, or lack of them, appropriate to those times.

The Old Testament was then the only primal, historical light that shone in the darkness, for apart from it (at that time) we were not in possession of history written earlier than 1000 BC. Light concerning early civilizations began to dawn when A. H. Layard and P. E. Botta commenced uncovering the sites near Nineveh, but the discoveries there did not at the time take us back to the times of Abraham; later they reached the times of the Flood and beyond. Yet notwithstanding all this modern research many modern scholars have not abandoned theories, now wholly untendable, that had been constructed upon the earlier obsolete assumptions.

The Second Reason

Their basic mistake was that they attempted a literary analysis of the book of Genesis, resting on differences of style and the use of special words and phrases, at a time when ancient literary methods were unknown. Any competent estimate of the age, compostion, or authorship of a book implies a wide and adequate knowledge of the literary method in use during the period covered by the book. But the higher-critical theories were advanced before anyone was in possession of a single secular document of the patriarchal age, and the critics were thus wholly ignorant of the manner in which records of that age were written. When this is understood, it is not surprising to read in J. Wellhausen's account of the inception and growth of this literary analysis, about "conjectures," or of the way successive critics scrapped not only the conclusions but the principles on which their predecessors had based their theories. Thus the "two document theory" was contradicted by the "supplementary hypothesis," and this in its turn was displaced by the "crystallisation hypothesis." Like men groping in the dark, advanced scholars wove together their intermixture of short-lived theories. At last Wellhausen wrote of "inconsistency," "reaction," "had really gone too far," "the fragmentary hypothesis was now superseded," this fragmentary theory "remained dominant till Hupfeld denied" and "his (Hupfeld's) assumption was corrected by Noldeck."

With such scanty critical apparatus, and without a single piece of writing from the age of Genesis to assist them, they commenced their analysis, finally dissecting Genesis into a series of unknown writers and editors all of whom they allege could be detected by their "style" or "editorial comments." Although nothing was known at this time, apart from Genesis, of early civilizations, these scholars assumed that the times must be excessively crude, yet they committed the fallacy of subjecting Genesis to a type of contemporary literary analysis, just as if it were a piece of modern writing.

The Third Reason

This lack of knowledge regarding early history made it possible for the critics to assume that civilization was primitive, and writing almost unknown to the patriarchs. So unenlightened were most of the workers at this time, it was imagined that the wedge-shaped writing which had been found, was only a form of pottery decoration. Until the mounds of Babylonia gave up their tens of thousands of tablets, and these, together with the inscriptions from the land of Egypt, had been deciphered, it was customary for commentators on Genesis to write a special introduction which defensively suggested that writing was sufficiently prevalent to enable Moses to write! Thus the conservative *Speakers' Commentary* issued in 1871 says on page two: "The first question then which naturally occurs is, was the art of writing known so early as Moses? and especially was it known to the Egyptians and the Jews?" As described above, it is now known that writing was so common a thousand years before the great lawgiver was born as to be used for ordinary commercial transactions. Civilization had already reached an advanced stage.

Similarly, theories concerning "myths" were adopted fifty years before the commencement of modern archaeological research. It was at the end of the eighteenth century, very soon after the "higher critics" had begun to formulate their theories, that there swept over Europe a literary fashion which attempted to label as myth all early history which has come down to us. In 1795 G. F. Wolf published his famous *Prolegomena*, in which he endeavored to show that the persons and places referred to by Homer were wholly mythological. He even denied that Homer had any existence. This craze spread like an epidemic and scholars everywhere occupied themselves with finding mythological explanations to account for historical facts. This method of interpretation was instantly taken up by the critical school, who endeavored to explain the historial facts of Genesis as "nature myth stories." However, in 1874, H. Schliemann began his excavations, and on the 16th November, 1876, he found the tomb of Agamemnon. His find was at first derided, for had not scholars decided that Agamemnon, King of Mycenae, was merely a mythical creation of an unknown Greek writer? But gradually, yet completely, the obvious facts of archaeology undermined this fourth pillar of criticism until it collapsed. The very mummies of so-called mythical and legendary figures and the palaces in which they lived have been unearthed.

It is therefore as unscientific as it is inaccurate to speak of "the assured results of modern criticism," for these results are neither asssured nor modern. Archaeology has given us the literary background of the patriarchal age, and a clear insight into the diffusion of civilizations and writing in those early times. Excavation has proved the critical theories to be not only groundless but false. The Bible statements have been abundantly confirmed.[1]

---

[1] The same can be argued for other aspects of ancient Near Eastern history. Gilgamesh the hero of a number of Babylonian epics, and once considered a merely legendary figure, has now been identified from named inscriptions as the ruler and restorer of the city of Erech, *ca.* 2600 BC.

X

Genesis Defends Itself

At this point we need to examine in greater detail the charges made by some critical scholars against the book of Genesis. These are:

(1) Differences in phraseology and style.

(2) Repetition of the same event.

(3) Evidences of date.

(4) Differing names for God.

Differences of Style

Some critics affirm that they can detect differences of phraseology and style in the book. They say that they are able to disjoin and isolate not only verses but phrases, and to distribute them among writers respectively called "Priestly," "Jehovist," "Elohist," etc. They assert their ability to discover where and when an editor or redactor has amended or added a single word. It is significant that, although they claim to know the literary style of these writers, they do not know their names or when or where they lived. In fact, this is the theory that presently holds the field: instead of merely one "Priestly" and one "Jehovist" writer, the book was composed by a school of writers, and their composition was spread over a considerable period. They add that the writings of this group were subjected to the scrutiny of several editors who endeavored to harmonize the narratives, and that the efforts of these editors received the attention of a final editor who scrutinized their work and gave the book the form it now possesses. They were forced to introduce this final editor. The admission is, however, fatal to their theory, for he would most certainly have been capable of eliminating any discrepancies or repetition had he seen them to exist. The least we can assume is that a Hebrew literary editor would have been as capable of detecting a discrepancy as the average modern scholar.

It would be wearisome to follow these writers through the confused maze of their examples of "differences of style and wording." If we take one simple narrative, Genesis 37, as an instance of this pretentious literary dissection, we find that they have distributed this single chapter in the following manner between three writers E, J, and P:

Verses 1—2a	assigned to P
2b—4	assigned to J
5—11	assigned to E
12—18	assigned to J
19—20	assigned to E
21	assigned to J
22—25a	assigned to E
25b—27	assigned to J
28a	assigned to E
28b	assigned to J
28c—30	assigned to E
31—35	assigned to J
36	assigned to E

According to this analysis the chapter becomes a tangle in which the products of "schools of writers" have been worked in alternately, yet the result is a continuous narrative. It has been shown above (in Chapters 5 to 8) that Moses plainly indicates the sources from which Genesis was compiled, and this is a sufficient answer to this critical medley of unknown schools of writers. It disposes of the intricate theories and assumptions that would assign it in fragments to unknown persons, who lived in unknown times, and at unknown places, yet about whom these scholars claim to know with infallible certainty their "style," "vocabulary," and religious opinions.

Repetition

The second series of charges made against Genesis is that there are many instances of "duplicate accounts." Dr. S. R. Driver writes, "the narrative of the Deluge, 6:9-13 (the wickedness of the earth) is a duplicate of 6:5-8." That such a repetition should exist is certainly significant, particularly that one should follow the other. What we believe to be the true significance of it has been referred to in Chapter 7, where it was observed that the first account (6:5-8) is the end of Noah's tablet, and the second (verses 9-13) commenced the history of the Flood written by the "sons of Noah." Moreover, such a repetition was a common literary method in early writing, and as the records contained in the early chapters of Genesis would require several tablets, it served to connect the record left by the sons of Noah with that written by Noah himself.

The next alleged duplicate is said to be contained in the two promises made to Sarah of a son in 17:16-19 and 18:9-15. This too, is quite naturally explained when we realize that we have in this section the tablets of both Isaac and Ishmael. Many theologians do not seem to realize that this charge of "repetition" could be brought against nearly every piece of ancient writing. It is characteristic of the style of the time and is evidence of their ancient character. In this connection Professor Arno Poebel in his work on cuneiform *Historical Texts*, issued by the University of Pennsylvania in 1914 (in commenting on some ancient Sumerian tablets found at Nippur), writes: "the readers of the Bible, moreover, will recognise the quaint principle of partial repetition or paraphrase."

The third instance quoted by S. R. Driver is that "The section 27:46 to 28:9 differs appreciably in style from 27:1-45." Again significantly enough these two passages are found in the section where we have the records of two persons, Isaac and Ishmael. It is not suggested by Dr. Driver that there is any discrepancy between them. That one should emphasize the side of Isaac and the other that of Ishmael is just what we should expect.

The fourth and fifth instances of S. R. Driver's criticism in 28:19 and 35:15 are: "we find two explanations of the name Bethel, and two explanations of the name of Israel in 32:28 and 35:10. Esau is described as already resident in Edom, whereas in 36:6, his migration there is attributed to causes which could not have come into operation until after Jacob's return to Canaan" (*Genesis*). This criticism is presumably based on the assumption that Esau had no cattle until after Jacob's return from Padan-aram. But Jacob did not go away to Padan-aram until he was 77; there is not a word in this passage which could be said to be in the slightest degree improbable. Surely S. R. Driver was aware that Mount Seir is only at the southern end of the Dea Sea, and that Jacob was living at Beersheba, merely fifty miles away. Modern scholars constantly speak of these patriarchs as nomad sheiks. A return to Canaan and a subsequent parting would not be abnormal. I submit that no difficulty exists.

Having dealt with all the alleged duplicate passages

and differences of explanation that this leading modern
critic makes on Genesis, I leave the reader to judge between Genesis and critic.

Evidences of Date

The next line of attack relates to evidences of date, for
certain passages are alleged to indicate a date later than
Moses. In the words again of S. R. Driver:

> There are indeed passages in Genesis which cannot
> reasonably be supposed to have been written until after
> Israel had been settled in Canaan, as 12:6, 13:7, 14:14
> (Dan), 21:32, 34, and 26:1 (the Philistines, if what is
> stated on 10:14 is correct, were not in Palestine till the
> age of Rameses III, considerably after the Exodus),
> 36:31 (a verse which obviously presupposed the exis-
> tence of the monarchy in Israel), 40:15 (Canaan called the
> "land of the Hebrews") (*Genesis*).

As the first two passages refer to the same situation,
they may be taken together. In 12:6 we read, "and the
Canaanite was then in the land"; in 13:7, "and the Canaanite and the Perizzite dwelt then in the land." All the
difficulty vanishes if, as suggested, these sentences are
understood as explanations made by Moses when compiling Genesis from tablets. When the context is read
carefully, it will be seen that Moses is referring to the
two localities, Shechem and Bethel, where Abraham had
lived temporarily when first entering the land. When
Abraham arrived in Palestine from Mesopotamia he
pitched his tent at Shechem—then the Canaanite dwelt
in this district—and when he continued his journey
southwards to Bethel, he found "the Canaanite and the
Perizzite" were inhabitants of the district. Now it is evident by the use of the two names "Canaanite" and "Perizzite" that "Canaanite" is to be understood here as it
often is elsewhere, as merely one of the many tribes then

inhabiting Palestine. But these notes by Moses were not written until the people were on the margin of the land and about to enter it after forty years in the wilderness, that is, a period of over 400 years after Abraham's brief stay at Shechem and Bethel. What then was the differences in the habitation of these tribes between the times of Abraham and Moses? This is what Moses is indicating, and this we find from Numbers 13:29, where we read that in the days of Moses, "the Amorites dwell in the mountains and the Canaanites dwell by the sea and along by the side of the Jordan." Thus in the 400 years which had elapsed, the Canaanite had lost his foothold or had moved from the mountainous country around Shechem and Bethel to the lowlands along the seacoast and the Jordan valley. The canaanitish clans that the people would meet on entering these parts of the land had therefore changed, and Moses here has made a note to indicate that the inhabitants of Abraham's day are no longer living in the same places. The addition of these notes, therefore, is a clear attestation that the original was written in Abraham's or Isaac's time, and that the note explaining the new situation was later made by Moses.

The next objection concerns the word "Dan" in 14:14. Contemporary scholars assume that it refers to the town of Dan taken in the days of the Judges. This assumption cannot be proved or pressed; the scholars of ancient days would know as well as the critics of today the date when Laish was named "Dan." Such repetition of simple names is constantly occurring in ancient tablets, and no Assyrian scholar would jump to the conclusion that there was necessarily a contradiction. In all probability the reference was to an ancient town of this name in existence long before the person or town of Laish was taken by the tribe of Dan.

The next difficulty raised by S. R. Driver is one which

he himself admits to have made by his conjecture that the Philistines are referred to in 10:14. It is not a Bible difficulty, but one which his own supposition has created.

The final, and to the critical scholars the most decisive passage in Genesis, which they think to be indicative of the late date on which it was written, is in 36:31, where we read, "These are the kings of Edom before there reigned any king of Edom before there reigned any king over the children of Israel." Dr. Driver says of this verse that, "it obviously presupposes a monarchy in Israel," and, therefore, hints that it was written after Saul began to reign. The passage does not necessarily presuppose this, for it simply says, "reigned *over* the children of Israel," and not reigned *in* Israel. Pharaoh reigned over the children of Israel; while in Egypt the whole nation had become subjects of the king of Egypt. The opening verses of Exodus inform us that this sovereignty had become arbitrary and despotic, that they were then the slaves of Pharaoh who feared they may "fight, so as to get them up out of the land" (Exod. 1:10). In order to prevent their escape the king commanded that all male children born should be put to death. They said of themselves that they were Pharaoh's bondmen. This phrase "before there reigned any king over Israel" is a note of explanation, as all are agreed, but who is more likely than Moses to have written it? He knew of Pharaoh's reigning over Israel. But there is a further reference. In Deuteronomy 7:8 we are told that the "Lord brought you out with a mighty hand and redeemed you out of the house of bondage, from the hand of Pharaoh." In the song of Moses the princes of Edom and kingship are again mentioned together. After the overthrow of Pharaoh in the sea we read, "the Dukes of Edom shall be amazed....The Lord shall reign for ever and ever," and in the final poem written just before he died (Deuteronomy

33), Moses speaks of the God of Jeshurun being king in Jeshurun (i.e. Israel). We have already seen that it was just at this period of his life that Moses wrote some of these "notes of explanation."

Further evidence that this list of Edomite kings ended at the time Moses wrote, is to be found in the fact that, when 1 Chronicles 1 repeats this list from Genesis 36, it adds one phrase about the last king, Hadar: "he died." In Genesis this fact is recorded of all the kings named before Hadar, so it would appear that he was still living in Moses' day. But S. R. Driver makes much of this "difficulty," and referring to the list of kings who reigned over Edom he writes, "the last-mentioned king will actually live just before the time of Saul." But nearly 800 years elapsed between the date of Esau's marriage and "the time of Saul," and this would involve eight kings reigning for 800 years. To such lengths will such a scholar go to support what he and the critics maintain to be the most decisive argument indicating a late date. In those days eighty years may well have been ample for eight kings to reign, as none of their sons succeeded to the kingship. Ninety years elapsed between Esau's marriage and Jacob going down to Egypt, and 250 years more before Moses arrived at the edge of the land of Canaan, in all a period of 340 years. It is more than sufficient time for eight kings to hold power over a clan. Yet there is scarcely a critical attack on Genesis which does not assert this so-called "difficulty" to be overwhelming. On such trivial grounds has the authenticity of Genesis been questioned.

We have examined this expert witness, and have fairly and honestly endeavored to permit him to state his accusations in his own words, nothing relevant being omitted. His charges have been considered and, it is submitted, disposed of completely. The one-sided nature of the evidence given by this witness is apparent when it is seen that he has merely brought forward statements which he thinks tell against the book being a true and ancient history. On the other hand he has omitted in his summary every passage that speaks in its defense. In this paragraph of S. R. Driver's regarding "evidences of date," he says nothing whatever about such a verse as Genesis 10:19, which refers to Sodom and Gomorrah as towns then in existence, and refers to them as a landmark, notwithstanding that these cities were destroyed beyond recognition as early as Abraham's day. He does not similarly deduce from this verse that it must have been written before the days of Abraham, when they were destroyed. When the poverty of the critical case against Genesis is compared with the overwhelming evidence the book provides in its own defense, the verdict must surely be certain.

One remaining critical objection, that of the use of the divine names, is dealt with in the following chapter.

XI

The Titles for God

The chief imputation made against Genesis by modern scholars is that different names for the Almighty are used in various parts of the book. Each different writer, they allege, had only one name for God. On this assumption they endeavor to account for the use of different names, by asserting that each section or verse where a particular divine name is mentioned, indicates that it was written by the writer who uses that name exclusively or predominantly. It was on the basis of this use of the divine name in Genesis that modern scholars first elaborated their theories, until at length they represented the book as a piece of literary patchwork, and extended their application to the remaining books of the Old Testament. As the critical "documentary theory" of the composition of Genesis originated in the supposed exclusive use by one writer of the name of Jehovah (or Yahweh, AV the LORD), this document theory and the use of the name Jehovah will be considered together in this chapter.

Astruc's Theory

It was Jean Astruc, a French physician, who invented the theory of separate documents based on these divine names. He found that in the first thirty-five verses of

Genesis, that is, 1—2:4a, the word "Elohim" (God) was used and no other divine name, while in chapters 2:4b—3:24 the only designation given is "Jehovah Elohim" (Lord God), except where Satan uses the word God. The passages must have been written by different writers, he said, for if Moses wrote the whole of it himself first-hand, then he would have to attribute to him this singular variation, in patches, of the divine name. He then divided the book up into little sections according to the divine name used. Thus he alleged that a writer who used "Elohim" was the author of the Elohist document, and the writer who used "Jehovah" was called the "Jehovist." As this two-fold theory was found to fail as an explanation, seeing that some verses which were obviously written by the same person contained both names for God, another contrivance was devised in order to separate the verse into two parts. This was done by introducing an editor, who combined these two documents into one. Even this complication did not satisfy, for the modern scholars had to admit that the word "Elohim" (God) appeared in passages which they attributed to the writer who was supposed to use the name "Jehovah" exclusively. A loophole out of this difficulty was soon devised by alleging another "redactor," who has altered the divine names.

After a century of such conjectures the following elaborate tangle had been produced to explain the use of "Jehovah" and "Elohim" in Genesis. Two different writers, or rather schools of writers, some time after the reign of Saul, produced two documents known as "J" and "E." A redactor called "RJE" combined these two documents into one. In the course of his editing he is supposed to have taken pieces from "J" then "E," sometimes altering, at other times adding a passage of his own. It is asserted that this editor has done his work so well that it is difficult to separate the original writings. Another redactor revised and again altered this composition. It is then said that a further document was written nearly a thousand years after Moses, called "P," and a redactor called "EP" added this document to "JE," inserting details of his own authorship. In this way Genesis has been reduced to a series of confused fragments and authors, in order to account for the way the name of God is used in the book. At times the critics assert that the Bible was written just like all other books. But no other book was ever written in this fashion! Some years ago a critical edition of Genesis was issued in which the parts written by these alleged authors and editors were represented in inks of various colors; it became known as the "Rainbow Bible." J. Skinner's volume on *The Divine Names in Genesis* is an illustration of the tangle into which this subject has been tied. The critical scholars have to admit that their literary expedients break not only the logical but also the grammatical sequence of passages; it is confusion confounded. J. Wellhausen acknowledged that the result was an "agglomeration of fragments."

But J. Astruc had found one important verse of Scripture to which he appealed in support of his theory, and all the succeeding workers have made this the foundation text of their arguments. In Exodus 6:3 we read, "I appeared unto Abraham, Isaac and Jacob, as God Almighty [El-Shaddai], but by my name Jehovah I was not known to them." This, it was said, is a clear and explicit statement. One leading scholar writes, "unless the writer of Exodus 6:3 contradicts himself not one of these passages [in Genesis] can have issued from his hands" (J. E. Carpenter, *Oxford Hexateuch*).

Alternative Explanations

On the other hand the defenders of Genesis most unreasonably dislike the modern scholars making their stand on this text of Scripture ("by my name Jehovah I was not known to them," Exod. 6:3). These scholars maintain that the verse cannot mean precisely what it appears to mean, because the name of Jehovah is in fact used nearly 200 times in Genesis. The usual explanation given for this by anti-critics is, "though the name was ancient and known to the Patriarchs, its *full meaning* was not known to them, and so God was not manifested to them by it," or "the name of Jehovah was known, but not known to be understood." These interpretations overlook first the fact that God distinctly states the alternative way by which he appeared to Abraham, Isaac, and Jacob, and secondly that there is no special explanation of the full meaning of the name, other than the simple yet profound declaration "I AM THAT I AM."

Further, in the endeavor to show that Exodus 6:3 cannot mean what it says, appeal is made to such passages as Genesis 4:26, "then began men to call upon the name of Jehovah." But it is found that the name occurs even before this, so for an instance, the editor of the *Companion Bible*, who was an anti-critic, says of this verse: "If this refers to Divine worship it is not true, for Abel and Cain both began, and their descendants doubtless followed their example. What was really begun, was the *profanation of the name of Jehovah*." This is just as much conjecture as that of the critical scholars, for the verse does not contain a hint of such a thing, and had this been the case it would have said so. Such evasions are pathetically ridiculous attempts to get out of a difficulty. Many similar unreasonable and unwarranted wriggles could be cited where commentators, in attempting to rid themselves of the perplexing passage, have abandoned the plain meaning of words.

A more elaborate, but even less convincing type of explanation is offered by that able Jewish scholar, H. M. Weiner, who writes:

Suffice it to say that in the opinion of the writer the reading "I made known" is clearly right. The meaning which at first sight appears to be the same, is seen, in the light of comparative evidence as to primitive ideas, to be absolutely different. It appears that men in a certain state of civilisation hold that names have an objective existence, and regard the utterance of a man's name by himself as giving his interlocutor a certain power over him. There is plenty of Old Testament evidence to show that the early Hebrews believed in the objective existence of names. It seems that here the utterance of the Name of God, not in any incidental or evasive fashion (as, for instance, in quotation, "Thus saith the Lord," etc., in Exod. 3:15), but as a part of the direct formula "I am the Lord," would have an esoteric meaning for the ancient Hebrew. The true effect of the phrase was not to reveal a new name or give a fresh meaning to an old one, but to create a bond between Deity and people, and to give Moses and the Israelites a direct pledge that the whole power of Deity would be exerted on their behalf (*Origins of the Pentateuch*).

A Fundamental Misconception

Numerous contradictory explanations have been given both by critics and defenders to account for the fact that in Exodus 6:3 we are told that God was not known to the patriarchs by the name of Jehovah, while on the other hand, Genesis frequently represents Abraham, Isaac, and Jacob, as using the name. *I submit that all these contradictory explanations and evasions have been due to the fundamental mistake made by both sides in assuming that no part of Genesis had been written until the time of Moses.* This crucial assumption has resulted in the desperate literary tangle of the modern scholars and the difficulties of the defenders. The critics find themselves in the hopeless position of employing numerous editors who had before them the explicit statement of Exodus 6:3, when they are said to have edited Genesis. Are we supposed to assume that the final editor was unaware that he was contradicting himself? The critical "explanations" only increase their difficulties.

All these evasions are made because neither side in this great and prolonged debate has realized that the book of Genesis is a record written by the persons whose names are stated in it, that the earlier writers used a primitive script, and that the later tablets were written in the cuneiform script and language of the day. There cannot be the slightest doubt that the tablets which Abraham would take with him from Ur of the Chaldees, would be written in the cuneiform script prevalent in that city. When Moses came into possession of these tablets he would find on some of them the cuneiform equivalent for "God." An instance of this may be seen in the tablet of Creation, where "God" is used thirty-four times, and no other divine title or name appears. In others he would find in addition the cuneiform equivalent of "El Shaddai" (God Almighty or All Sufficient), the name by which Exodus 6:3 plainly states he appeared to Abraham, Isaac, and Jacob.

The Importance of "El Shaddai"

There are some noteworthy facts regarding this word "Shaddai" to which sufficient attention has not been given. In the first place, the full composite title "El Shaddai" as stated in Exodus 6:3 is not used elsewhere than in Genesis, and these uses are on important occasions (Gen. 17:1, 28:3, 35:11, 48:3). The next impressive fact is that the word "Shaddai" alone is used forty-two times in almost every instance by persons writing or living outside Palestine, and in contact with Babylonian cuneiform modes of expression. Job uses it thirty-one times. Balaam who came from Mesopotamia, Naomi the Moabitess, and Ezekiel the prophet in Babylonia use it.

This accounts for thirty-eight of the forty-two uses of the word and is surely significant.

We have an account in Exodus 3 of God's revelation of himself to Moses at Horeb, and of Moses' commission to go down into Egypt to bring up the people out of slavery:

> And Moses said unto God, Behold, when I come unto the children of Israel, and shall say unto them, The God of your fathers hath sent me unto you; and they shall say to me, *What is his name?* What shall I say unto them? And God said unto Moses, I AM THAT I AM: and he said, Thus shalt thou say unto the children of Israel, I AM hath sent me unto you. And God said moreover unto Moses, Thus shalt thou say unto the children of Israel, Jehovah, the God of your fathers, the God of Abraham, the God of Isaac, the God of Jacob, hath sent me unto you, this is my name for ever.

It is necessary at this juncture to note the difference between a *name* and a *title*. The word "God" is not a *name*, it is a title. Jehovah was the *name* of God. This distinction may be seen in the second commandment: "Thou shalt not take the *name* of *Jehovah* thy God in vain." The Jew did not mind writing and speaking of God (Elohim). However, he so regarded this commandment that he did not utter the name Jehovah when reading the Scriptures but substituted the word "Adonai" for it. Moreover, the Hebrews spoke of *the* Elohim, the true God, as contrasted with false gods, but never did they speak or write of *the* Jehovah, for there was only one Jehovah in heaven and earth. In Genesis we read of "my God," but never of the "Jehovah of Israel," for there was only one Jehovah. I do not stay to enter into the question of the exact pronouncation of the name. God says: "I am Jehovah, that is my name, and my glory I will not give to another, neither my praise to graven images."

When men began to make "gods many and lords many," they called them "gods"; but to distinguish them from each other, they gave each a *name*. Thus the word "god" ceased to be used, even in Scripture, exclusively of the Creator of the heavens and the earth. It is used for idols because we find Laban calling his teraphim which Rachael had stolen, "gods" (*elohim*), and Jacob does the same. In Exodus 12:12, we read of the "gods [*elohim*] of Egypt." Chemosh and Dagon are the names of, and are called, *elohim*. Babylonia had dozens of "gods," but each of them had a distinguishing name, as well as the title "god." The names of more than eighty Babylonian "gods" who were worshipped in the time of Abraham, and whose names have been found in tablets with the determinative *ilu* (god), may be seen in Dr. Herman Ranke's *Early Babylonian Personal Names of the Hammurabi Dynasty* published in series D of *Researches and Treatises of the University of Pennsylvania.*

When we reach the time of Moses, matters in this respect were even worse, for there were over forty petty states in Egypt, each with its own chief god, worshipped in the temple at the principal city of its name or state. All these gods had other gods associated with them, a wife goddess, or sons called "gods," and each in his own territory was regarded as a "god almighty" and as the creator and preserver of all the world and people. The Egyptian seemed to see nothing illogical in these scores of gods, each being creator and ruler of the world. All of them were given names to distinguish them from each other. Besides this, each town and village possessed its own god. The Theban Recension of the "Book of the Dead" gives the names of over 450 gods, and the pyramid texts contain references to over 200. Although the names of many of the Egyptian gods have been lost to us, those of over 2,200 are known. Amidst all this polytheism it became necessary, when God was to reveal himself (as he did in Exodus 6) in a special manner both to the Hebrews and to the Egyptians, that he should use a *name* to distinguish himself, the only true God, from all the false gods around. That name was a most significant one, "I AM."

The Problem for Moses

When Moses, at a later date than the revelation of Exodus 6, was compiling the book of Genesis, with his patriarchal tablets before him, he would find the cuneiform equivalent of El Shaddai on many of them. Now that God had given himself a new name, Jehovah (a personal pronoun, not a title), which word for God should he use in transcribing these ancient tablets? Every translator of the Bible has been confronted with the same problem. The title "God" may be repeated, but how is the description or name—the cuneiform equivalent of El Shaddai— to be transcribed where necessary, unless the new revealed name of God (that is Jehovah) is used? To use any other name would be to create a misunderstanding in the minds of those for whom Genesis was being prepared.

The translators of the Bible into Chinese had the same problem. Which of the Chinese names should be used? *Tien-chu*, meaning "the Lord of heaven," or *Shang-ti*, the Confucian name for the "Supreme Ruler," or *Shin* which may mean "spirit." If there had been a pure name of description for "God" in China, a name not debased by association with the religions of the country, there would have been no difficulty. In Arabic-speaking countries, the word *Allah* is used for the one God in heaven. The singular of Elohim is *Elah*, in the Arabic it is *ilah*, and with the article *al'ilah* the modern equivalent of *Allah*. This is a good Arabic title for God, but if I speak of Allah to a Christian or a Jew, living in an Arabic-speaking country, I at once associate myself with Mohammedanism.

What name then was Moses to write? God had revealed himself to him by the name of Jehovah, and that name had been announced to the children of Israel in Egypt and was revered by them. Now that the ancient records of their race, preserved in purity and handed down by Abraham, Isaac, and Jacob, were being edited and possibly translated by Moses, what name should he use? He saw that the ancient title "El Shaddai," God Almighty or All Sufficient, had been corrupted by its use in connection with scores of other "gods," each of whom were called "god almighty" by their devotees? The most natural course was to use the name Jehovah. Thus then, is the presence of the word Jehovah in Genesis quite naturally explained. It is not by assuming a complicated jumble of tangled documents written by unknown writers as the modern scholars do, or by an evasion of the literal meaning of Exodus 6:3, but by the inspiration from God which led Moses in most instances to translate "El Shaddai" by the word Jehovah—his distinguishing name, that separated him from the heathen gods around.

God's Name on the Tablets

When it is understood, as explained in earlier chapters, that Genesis is composed of a series of tablets as indicated by the formula, "These are the origins of...," it will be seen that it aids in a most significant way in explaining the remarkable use of the name and title given to Jehovah God. In our survey of the first tablet we saw that the only divine name on it was "God," also that the contents of this tablet were a personal revelation to Adam. At the dawn of history it was sufficient to use the name "God," for at that time there were no other "gods," so that a name in addition to a title was obviously unnecessary in the first tablet.

The second tablet (2:4b—4:26), written, as we noticed, before the beginning of the Flood, contains both the title "God," and the name "Jehovah." In this tablet the name and title are always used together except by the tempter and Eve, and this exclusive combined use is peculiar to this tablet. Is not this due to the revelation given during this period, of the cuneiform equivalent of the title El Shaddai, now translated Jehovah? It was of the days of Adam's grandson, Enosh, that we read, "then began men to call upon the name of Jehovah." Hence, in this tablet, we have both a name and a title for God, for the most probable reason that at this time men began to worship other gods, so that then a distinguishing name became a necessity.

The writer of this book came to Genesis simply to find its natural divisions, and discovered that by adhering to the proper use of the formula, "These are the origins of...," the book revealed its own original records, and thereafter the critical difficulties, especially those connected with the use of the name and title for God, were seen to be without support.

XII

Jesus and the
New Testament Authors

There can be no doubt whatever that the writers of the New Testament so believed the statements recorded in the book of Genesis that they made its narratives the basis on which some of the most important doctrinal statements of Christianity are founded.

The Attitude of Jesus

Critical scholars are unanimous that there is one person whose witness about Genesis always tells against them. They realize that their theories collapse unless the value of his testimony regarding Genesis is discredited. There is no attempt to question the kind of evidence our Lord Jesus Christ gives; they admit that his statements are opposed to their own, so two theories have been invented which result in refusing to admit him as a reliable witness. These are the "accommodation" and the "kenosis" theories. It is doubtful if they would have seen the light of day had not the critics seen that their theories were opposed to his plain statements. The effect of the first theory is to deny his truthfulness, and of the second, his knowledge.

The Accommodation Theory

The first implies that even if he believed the book of
Genesis to be a literary patchwork by unknown authors
who lived long after the time of Moses, he would speak
to the people in such a manner as to lead them to believe
that Moses wrote it. In other words they allege that he
accommodated himself to the errors he found around
him. It is sufficient to say that he spent his public minis-
try cutting clean across the prevailing ideas and errors
of his time; there is not the slightest evidence whatever
for the theory. It implies that Christ knew that Moses
had little or nothing to do with the early books of the
Old Testament, that, for instance, such a Flood as described therein had never occurred but that he accommodated his speech to the ideas of the people who believed
in the narratives of Genesis. Yet the astounding thing is
that these very critics often say that when preaching or
writing about Genesis they themselves cannot be absolutely honest unless they indicate that they have no be-
lief in the literal fact or accuracy of these records. This
surely implies that they feel they themselves must maintain a higher degree of honesty than they attribute to
the Lord.

The Kenosis Theory

The second or "kenosis" theory in effect asserts that
our Lord did not know as much as the modern critic does
about the book of Genesis. A critical Bible dictionary of
the moderate school may be cited here: "Both Christ and
his Apostles or writers of the New Testament held the
current Jewish notions respecting the Divine authority
and revelation of the Old Testament" (Hastings, *Dictionary of the Bible*). This dictionary maintains that these

"current Jewish notions" were wholly unreliable. The consequence of this is that the reliability of Christ is more insidiously undermined. They say that he may be relied upon for religious facts but that his references to authorship or to certain narratives of the Old Testament cannot be relied on. On the other hand he said, "If I have told you earthly things and ye believe not how shall ye believe if I tell you heavenly things?"

We find that our Lord Jesus Christ put his seal on the book of Genesis; the earlier chapters of it are most particularly, though incidentally, referred to by him. He quotes from the second chapter and also refers to the Creation account, to the Fall, to Satan, Abel, Noah, the Flood, and to Lot and the destruction of Sodom. We find that general or specific attestations are made to Genesis, chapters 1, 2, 3, 4, 5, 6 to 9, and 11, as well as to incidents in the lives of Abraham, Isaac, and Jacob as recorded in other chapters.

Let us examine this testimony in more detail. In Matthew 19:4-5 RV (also Mark 10:6-8) he refers to the creation of the human race: "He answered and said, Have ye not read, that he which made them from the beginning made them male and female, and said, For this cause shall a man leave his father and mother and shall cleave to his wife and they twain shall become one flesh"—a citation from Genesis 2:24.

He referred to Satan in John 8:44: "Ye are of your father the devil, and the lusts of your father it is your will to do. He was a murderer from the beginning, and stood not in the truth, because there is not truth in him. When he speaketh a lie he speaketh of his own; for he is a liar, and the father thereof." The reference here is evidently to Satan in the Garden of Eden.

An explicit reference to the beginning was made in Luke 11:50-51, when he said, "that the blood of all the prophets which was shed from the foundation of the world may be required of this generation; from the blood of Abel unto the blood of Zacharias."

He emphasized the lesson of Noah, the Ark, and the Flood in Luke 17:26-27: "And as it came to pass in the days of Noah, even so shall it be also in the days of the Son of Man. They ate, they drank, they married, they were given in marriage, until the day that Noah entered into the Ark, and the Flood came and destroyed them all." He then went on to speak of Lot and the destruction of Sodom (verse 28): "Likewise even as it came to pass in the days of Lot; they ate, they drank, they bought, they sold, they planted, they builded; but in the day that Lot went out from Sodom it rained fire and brimstone from heaven, and destroyed them all."

There is repeated mention of Abraham. Our Lord said, "Your father Abraham rejoiced to see my day; he saw it, and was glad. The Jews therefore said unto him, Thou art not yet fifty years old, and hast thou seen Abraham? Jesus said unto them, Verily, verily, before Abraham was, I am. They took up stones therefore to cast at him" (John 8:56-59). In referring to the patriarchs, he made it plain that though dead, they still had an existence, for he said, "God is not the God of the dead, but of the living." After the resurrection, "beginning from Moses and from the prophets, he interpreted to them in all the Scriptures the things concerning himself" (Luke 24:27). A few days later he said unto them, "These are my words which I spake unto you while I was yet with you, how that all things must needs be fulfilled which are written in the law of Moses and the prophets and the Psalms concerning me. Then opened he their understanding that they might understand the Scriptures" (Luke 24:44-45).

The New Testament Writers

Outstanding instances of this use of Genesis are those made by the apostle Paul in Romans 5 and 1 Corinthians 15. In Romans, he writes, "Wherefore as by one man sin entered into the world, and death by sin...nevertheless death reigned from Adam to Moses, even over them that had not sinned after the likeness of Adam's transgression." He continues the contrast between Adam and Christ, in the effect of Adam's sinful act in the Garden and Christ's righteous act on the Cross. If a person assumes Adam and the Fall to be merely myths, then the great result attributed in this passage to the Lord Jesus Christ, in dealing with the effects of that sin, is wholly negatived.

In the second passage (1 Cor. 15) Adam is referred to as the head of the human race, "For as in Adam all die, so in Christ shall all be made alive...so also it is written the first man Adam became a living soul, the last Adam became a life-giving Spirit...the first man is of the earth, earthy, the second man is the Lord from heaven." Reference is made to the Creation in 1 Timothy 2:12 and Hebrews 4:4. There can be no doubt that these passages are based upon the narratives of Genesis.

Paul, in 2 Corinthians 11:3, writes, "the serpent beguiled Eve through his subtilty." Hebrews 11:4 tells us how "by faith Abel offered unto God a more excellent sacrifice than Cain," and 1 John 3:12 says, "not as Cain who was of the wicked one and slew his brother. And wherefore slew he him? Because his works were evil and his brother's righteous." Jude writes that "Enoch the seventh from Adam prophesied," and Hebrews 11:7, that "By faith Noah, being warned of God concerning things not seen as yet, moved with godly fear, prepared an ark." Peter in his first epistle (3:20) refers to the time when "the longsuffering of God waited in the days of Noah, while the ark was preparing, wherein few, that is, eight souls were saved through water," and in his second epistle (2:5) he adds that God "spared not the ancient world, but preserved Noah with seven others, a preacher of righteousness, when he brought a flood upon the world of the ungodly."

References to Abraham

The outstanding passage in the New Testament illustrative of absolute faith in God, attributes that faith to Abraham. Genesis 15:6 reads, "And he believed in the Lord; and he counted it to him for righteousness." Not only Paul but James used this statement; they make it the basis of their discussion. Again in Romans 4:3, Paul appeals to this incident in the life of Abraham by asking, "For what saith the Scripture?" Then he quotes this verse from Genesis. Moreover, he also made it the foundation of his argument in his Galatian epistle. In addition, Stephen says (Acts 7:2): "The God of glory appeared unto our father Abraham, when he was in Mesopotamia, before he dwelt in Haran, and said to him, Get thee out of thy country, and from thy kindred, and come into the land which I shall shew thee. Then came he out of the land of the Chaldees." Unless we can rely upon the fact that Abraham actually lived and also that he acted with outstanding faith in God, these apostolic references are worse than useless for the purpose for which they are cited.

Other incidents in the life of Abraham are quoted as reliable history. In 2 Peter 2:6 we read that God "turning the cities of Sodom and Gomorrah into ashes condemned them with an overthrow, having made them an example unto those that should live ungodly." In a similar manner Jude also writes of these cities. Further, Hebrews (11:17) tells us that, "By faith Abraham, being

—140—

tried, offered up Isaac, yea, he that had gladly received the promises was offering up his only begotten son; even he to whom it was said, In Isaac shall thy seed be called: accounting that God is able to raise up, even from the dead"; and James writes, "And was not Abraham our father justified by works when he offered up Isaac on the altar?"

Other References

Other persons and incidents related in Genesis are quoted in the same definitely historical manner. Paul refers (Gal. 4:22-31) to Abraham's two sons Ishmael and Isaac, and to the "son of the bondwoman and the son of the freewoman." We read in Hebrews 11:20 that Isaac "blessed Jacob and Esau," and that "by faith Jacob, when he was dying, blessed each of the sons of Joseph, leaning upon the top of his staff"; and in the following chapter, of Esau selling his birthright and repenting of it. Stephen, in Acts 7, speaks of the way Jacob's sons "moved with jealousy against Joseph, sold him into Egypt; and God was with him and delivered him out of all his afflictions and gave him wisdom and favor before Pharaoh, King of Egypt; and he made him Governor over Egypt and all his house." This chapter also refers to the famine in Canaan and Jacob's moving down into Egypt. 2 Peter 2:7 refers to God having "delivered righteous Lot sore distressed by the lascivious life of the wicked." Hebrews 11:22 says "that Joseph when his end was nigh made mention of the departure of the children of Israel, and gave commandment concerning his bones."

Thus every prominent incident and person in Genesis is referred to in the New Testament, not merely in a vague and general way. They are introduced into the most decisive statements written. A scrutiny of these passages leaves upon the mind of the reader a most definite assurance that the apostles regarded these narratives of Genesis as real and inspired history. In fact, the New Testament has its historical roots in Genesis.

XIII

Conclusion

In Chapter 1 it was emphasized that adequate confirmation was necessary in order to establish the statement that the book of Genesis:

(1) Was originally written on tablets in an ancient script;

(2) By the patriarchs intimately acquainted with the events related;

(3) That Moses was the compiler of the book as we now have it;

(4) That he plainly directs attention to the sources of his information.

It is submitted that the confirmation given has been fully adequate, and the promise that it would be "attested by facts so numerous, and undesigned coincidences so overwhelming" has been amply fulfilled. Moreover, the corroboration presented is not of the subordinate kind that forms merely a number of separate links in a chain of evidences, the weakness in one link creating a weakness in the whole. It is rather a series of separate strands each strong in itself, but when woven together it produces a confirmation of such strength and substance that the weight of evidence requires a decision in favor of the contemporary writing of Genesis.

Summary of the Evidences

The various lines of evidence brought forward in these pages may be summarized as follows:

(1) Archaeological research (which commenced after "higher criticism" had produced its theories) has, in recent years, given us the ancient and contemporary background of Genesis, which agrees with its contents (Chapter 2).

(2) The Genesis narratives imply that rapid developments took place in early history. Archaeologists have dug down into virgin soil and found that a high state of culture existed in times previously called "prehistoric." They even assert that long before the time of Abraham, Sumerian civilization had reached its zenith (Chapter 3).

(3) As far back as archaeology has been able to go, and in the earliest times, examples of writing have been found. During the period covered by the greater part of Genesis, writing has been discovered to be in common use even for ordinary commerical transactions (Chapter 4).

(4) The contents of the earlier chapters of Genesis claim to have been written (Chapter 5).

(5) Both Scripture and archaeology give evidence that the narratives and genealogies of Genesis were originally written on stone or clay *tablets*, and in the ancient script of the time (Chapters 4 and 5).

(6) We now know something of the literary methods used by the ancients. Prominent among these was the colophon of the tablet. In our examination of Genesis we find a similar literary method, for the formula, "These are the origins of...," was the ancient conclusion which Moses inserted indicating the source from which he obtained the narratives and genealogies (Chapters 5 and 6).

(7) Other literary methods were the use of "titles" and "catchlines" in order to bring the tablets together in proper sequence. Although Genesis (as we know it) is a book compiled by Moses, there are still traces of the use of these literary means of preserving sequence (Chapter 6).

(8) In some instances indications are provided giving the date when the tablet was written. This is given in a most archaic way and very similar to the method prevailing in very ancient times (Chapter 6).

(9) In confirmation of (4) to (8) above, we have shown that in no instance is an event recorded that the person (or persons) named in chapter 5 could not have written from intimate personal knowledge, or have obtained absolutely unmistakable contemporary information. In Chapter 7 the positive evidence is reviewed showing that they were so written. The familiarity with which all the circumstances and details are described is noted.

(10) Additional corroboration is found in the significant fact that the history recorded in the sections written *over* the names of the patriarchs ceases in all instances on the date on which the tablet is stated to have been written or, where no date is given, before the death of that person. In most cases it is continued almost up to the date of the patriarch's death (Chapter 5).

(11) The presence of "Babylonian" words in the first eleven chapters is further evidence that the contents of the earliest narratives and genealogies were written during the lifetime of the early patriarchs of Genesis, for they used that language (Chapter 6).

(12) The presence of Egyptian words and Egyptian environment in the last fourteen chapters of Genesis adds its irresistible testimony that those chapters were written in Egypt (Chapter 6).

(13) The first tablet, that of the Creation, seems to

have been written at the very dawn of history. This is evidenced by its archaic expressions, for it was put into writing before names had been given to the sun and moon and before polytheism had arisen or clans developed (Chapter 7).

(14) There is no statement in Scripture to support the supposition that all the narratives and genealogies were handed down verbally; on the contrary, they claim to have been written down (Chapters 5, 7, and 8).

(15) Many references are made to towns which had either ceased to exist or whose original names are so ancient that the compiler had to insert the names by which they were known in his day. These new names and explanations fit in exactly with the circumstances of a people then on the edge of the land of Canaan, and about to enter it; thus indicating that Moses used earlier records and that he was the compiler of the book (Chapters 6 and 8).

(16) That Genesis should still contain archaic expressions and show traces of the literary aids associated with the use of clay tablets is a witness to the fidelity with which the text has been handed down to us (Chapter 6).

(17) It is clear that the ordinary Babylonian tablets of the Creation and the Flood are a corrupted form of the Genesis record. The narratives of Genesis are not merely a purified form of the Babylonian accounts (Chapter 2).

(18) Archaeology has completely undermined the "myth and legend" theory. Evidences of persons once thought by critics to be mythical have been discovered by archaeologists (Chapter 9).

(19) The difficulties alleged against Genesis by "higher critics" vanish quite naturally when it is understood that the narratives and genealogies were first written on tablets in an ancient script, by the persons whose names they bear, and that the book was compiled by Moses. Any differences of phraseology and style are just

what we should expect in these circumstances (Chapter 10).

(20) The "repetition of the same event," of which modern scholars speak, is shown to harmonize exactly with the arrangement of the tablets from which the book was composed and to conform to ancient Sumarian usage (Chapter 10).

(21) The outstanding examples brought forward by critics to suggest a late date for Genesis are shown to prove the reverse (Chapter 10).

(22) The documentary theory was originated in order to account for the use of the name Jehovah in Genesis and the exclusive use in certain sections (which we claim to have been tablets) of one particular name or title for God. On the basis of the documentary theory the unwieldy structure of "higher criticism" has been reared. It can, however, be shown that there are other possible explanations for the varying use of the divine names. This is especially the case when it is seen that in the book of Genesis we have contemporary and translated records (Chapter 11).

(23) The writers of the New Testament base important arguments and illustrations on the narratives of Genesis. These arguments and illustrations would be worse than useless—they would be misleading—unless these narratives rest on historical facts (Chapter 12).

(24) The testimony of our Lord Jesus Christ, the Son of God, to the narratives contained in Genesis is of greater value than all the preceding evidence and constitutes the pinnacle of these evidential verifications of its history. To the Christian mind the testimony of Christ must be decisive (Chapter 12).

These twenty-four strands woven together make a cumulative muster of evidences, so exceptional both in character and importance, that they establish the antiquity of Genesis as a contemporary record of events upon a sure foundation. This foundation is the internal testimony of the book itself, supported by the external corroboration of archaeology.